Synchronicity

Unlock Your Divine Destiny

By Amelía Aeon Karris

ISBN-13: 978-0692954577 (Know the Self)
ISBN-10: 0692954570

CREATIVE TEAM

Cover illustration: Max S. (Copyright) 2015-2017 (www.crypted99.deviantart.com)
Editing: Cynthia Cavalcanti, Robyn Fountain, Adam Jacobowitz, Grace Kerina and Chet Turnbeaugh
Author photos: Robin Clark Photography (back cover), Hyunah Jang (inside)
Graphic Illustrations: Nomita Khatri (workbook & diagrams), Kristin Groener (self mastery icons)

To Yamada-san, Eiko-chan, and my father, David, whose lives impacted me greatly, and to all the kind souls who supported me on this journey and illuminated my path.

May all beings return to love.
May all beings be liberated from fear.

Know the Self

A Mystery School for Modern Day Living

Table of Contents

The Shift Has Hit the Fan!

"It is no measure of health to be well adjusted to a profoundly sick society."
–Jiddu Krishnamurti

Have you settled for less, compromised yourself, or perhaps plain given up on your dreams? Do you find yourself asking, is this all there is to life? Perhaps you feel a constant sense of uneasiness—or maybe you've lost your childhood wonder and your adventurous spirit altogether?

Over the past ten years, as a sustainable lifestyle designer and a spiritual guide, I have offered my gifts to people around the world who are in the midst of a spiritual crisis, who are awakening to paranormal phenomena, and who are managing the aftermath of the inter-dimensional shift that hit the fan. My work is to help them stabilize their awakening and master their energy. My clients and students typically find me through highly synchronistic chains of events, just as they are ready to awaken to an entirely new paradigm. At other times, Spirit connects me with those who are in the midst of tumultuous changes and are needing to piece themselves, and their reality, back together.

The people with whom I work are often overwhelmed in their busy lives, at a crossroads facing a major decision, or simply feeling tired and beaten down by illness, trauma, setbacks, or recurring patterns. This overwhelm is a common theme that we all face at one time or another. Life can be confusing with all the demands to keep paying the rent or mortgage and to keep food on the table. How did our lives become so consumed with mere survival that we have forsaken our own connection to our spiritual nature? What are we so busy doing that we are missing the joy of life altogether?

Wherever you are right now in your life is perfect. It may not feel perfect, but it's exactly what it needs to be simply because it is. So often we have the "grass is greener" syndrome, thinking happiness lies outside ourselves somewhere, out there where everyone else is.

It pains me to see people chronically tired, depressed, sad, stressed, and struggling. Why are we struggling so much? Why is it that some of the poorest people on the planet are happier than many of the wealthiest? I've noticed that people who live close to the Earth seem to trust life more and enjoy relaxing. They know how to be still and sit with nature, how to hang out with others and be silent. What I find in the urban environments around the world is that most people have actually lost their ability to truly relax and be at ease with themselves. There is a program running that tells them they need to be busy and productive at all times. The idea of relaxation is often to sit in front of a T.V. or numb out with various substances such as alcohol, drugs, or sugar. It is like we have lost the ability to simply be still and be at peace with ourselves and the world around us.

Why are some of us more resilient than others? When life throws a hand grenade your way, do you get back up and dust yourself off in the aftermath of the destruction all around you? Or do you struggle for long periods in pain, depression, and exhaustion, thinking you will never recover?

In 2015, after I lost my house in a devastating fire, many people commented on my positive attitude and outlook on life. I was able to remain positive, despite the massive challenges, because inside I knew I was being carried somewhere better—even though it was impossible to see where that might be. The weeks leading up to the fire, during the fire, and the weeks that followed were all jam-packed with synchronistic events. These synchronicities allowed me to let go and trust where the river of life was taking me. We are handed lessons in order to build our inner strength, and we are never handed anything we cannot surmount or rise up and face.

Life is full of challenges. We can fall victim to our challenges, or we can rise up and meet them, and in so doing develop stamina, character, and deeper meaning. We can flow with life's current, or we can resist it.

Each of us is on a divine assignment that is connected to our ideal, our heart's deepest longing. By following the path of synchronicity, we can align with our destiny and live a life full of meaning.

Synchronicity is the awareness of an unseen hand orchestrating our life, directing us toward signs, symbols, messages, and encounters that are cosmic breadcrumbs to keep us on our heart's path.

Synchronicity gives us the feeling that there is a bigger tapestry that we are all a part of, and synchronistic moments allow us to see, if only briefly, those golden threads which stitch everything together.

Regardless of your beliefs, synchronistic events happen to everyone. They may appear in dramatic ways that usher in big changes, or they may appear as small, subtle, yet significant signs to guide you onto the path. Those who believe in God will call synchronicity the work of God, or an angel's message, though there is no need for us to discuss religion here. As you experience synchronicity, you will come to realize the very fabric of life and the spiritual science behind the tapestry. Anyone can tap into this phenomenon and experience it operating in their life.

We find spiritual science in the basic truth of our indigenous peoples; their understanding of life is simple. When you know these three simple truths, synchronicity abounds:

1.   All that is, is alive.
2.   All that is alive has Spirit.
3.   Everything is connected to everything else.

The goal of this book is to liberate you from your own self-destructive patterns, and to teach you how to flow with the river of life toward your divine destiny. Contained within these pages are practices for Self-actualization. The Self—with a capital "S'"—is the part of you that is your immortal presence. It is your true, authentic, and unchanging nature.

There are three levels on which we need to actualize our Self: the level of the personality (understanding why you act the way you do), the level of the soul (awakening to your authentic unchanging nature), and the level of the spirit (awakening to your divine assignment).

There is a complex science behind the simple keys I offer in this book, but there is no reason to get caught up in trying to be an electrician, much less a physicist, when all you need to do is flip a switch on. These practices will teach you how to turn on your lights and allow your soul's magic to illuminate your life.

We are living at a time in history when Ascended Masters, yogis, and modern-day mystics walk among us. People all over the world are waking up to their human potential, and it is now within reach of society as a whole to awaken to an entirely new state of consciousness.

As we surf the edge between the old paradigm and the new, we will learn to restore harmony within ourselves. Whether you know it or not, your soul has come here at this particular time both to witness and to participate in the events unfolding all around us. This is the time for which your soul has been preparing, and a time you have come to Earth to participate.

By practicing the Seven Keys I have outlined in this book, you will be able to anchor your soul's essence in your earthly body and remember your divine assignment as one of the New Earth architects. The New Earth is not a destination, or a place out in space. It is a state of consciousness and a palpable perception of a collective field that opens only to those who have awakened their multi-dimensional Self and are in service to the greater good. Together, we will lay the foundation of the New Earth and participate in the magic as it unfolds. I am so happy you are here! We need you to remember!

To get the most out of this book, I suggest you give each key ample time to fully integrate into your energetic system. This may take a few days, a week, or longer. Go at the pace your soul is ready to master. Return to the practices outlined here again and again for extraordinary results.

I have created a Companion Workbook to walk you step by step through the exercises I describe in the Seven Keys. Take a moment to download this valuable resource. You will also have access to audio and video files to guide you further. Go to **KnowTheSelf.com/workbook** to get access to all of these additional resources.

Puzzle Piece

Cut out perfectly from the Divine Design;

Scattered across worlds and universes;

Drawn like a magnet into Rightful Position;

Flowing on an unseen thread...

Weaving, Dodging, Nudging the other pieces

Bumping, Scraping, Colliding...testing the space

Do I fit here?

Moving, Shifting, Transforming

Voilá I fit!

I AM here!

I AM home!

I AM ME, I AM WE

I AM that puzzle piece I AM

— Annahkalayah

Key #1
Tend Your Inner Garden

*"Your heart is the light of this world.
Don't cover it with your mind."*
– Mooji

Since you are reading this book, I imagine you've had experiences with "meaningful coincidences," or what Carl Jung referred to as "synchronicity." Maybe you've asked yourself, what is synchronicity about, and why is it happening? You might have wondered, how do I follow these mysterious signs and symbols, and where are they leading me? Or perhaps you're in awe of the magic of synchronistic events and just want more of it.

As I mentioned earlier, you are here on a divine assignment. While you may not know what your mission is, your Spirit knows, and it is actively working to guide you onto your unique path. Synchronicity—the occurrence of remarkable "coincidences" that show up in your life—is your Spirit's way of ensuring you get the message, though the signs and symbols are not always clear or easy to interpret. As synchronicity becomes undeniably evident in your life, you may find yourself feeling confused, paranoid, or as if you're plain going crazy. Suddenly, you are faced with information that challenges your ideas about reality, arising through strange events and chance encounters as if in a dream––all despite the fact that you are fully awake and moving about through your day!

Synchronicity has been my compass since early childhood. I have rarely adhered to a moral code based on so-called right and wrong, and I have not always thought my way through life's decisions to find the "correct solution." Rather, I have followed synchronicity's unpredictable trail, and it has allowed me to successfully navigate an enormous number of challenges and golden opportunities. Time and again, synchronicity brought me into direct contact with people who shared critical gifts and messages at key points to shape my life and direct my destiny.

By following synchronicity's breadcrumbs, I have been led to personal mentors, mystics, yogis, shamans, and leading spiritual figures. I've been led to significant relationships and partnerships, each of which, when viewed from the conventional rational perspective, would appear as inexplicable as the next. By learning to read the signs and symbols, I have launched businesses in such diverse arenas as fashion, entertainment, technology, organic farming, sustainable community development, and now, the healing arts.

Synchronicity is not at all rational. It has directed me to pick up my roots and move abroad for a year to England, and then the Holy Land for six months (I am not Jewish, so that made no sense). Synchronistic events led me to work and reside for several years in Tokyo, Kyoto, and Mt. Fuji, opening magical doorways at every turn. It then directed me for eight long and magical years to settle in and among the sacred sites of Southern India. It later directed me to return to my homeland and the ancient Redwood forests of Northern California. Most recently, I was brought to live at the foot of Mount Shasta, one of the most intensely energetic places on the planet. None of these journeys made sense at the time.

As I attune to synchronicity, the messages generally increase in frequency and at an accelerating rate. When I've chosen to ignore them, they inevitably become louder and more forceful. I can tell you from personal experience, the more you listen to your intuition, the more magical and generous your life will become. And––and here's the great news—the more you work to *attune* your intuition, in part by learning to interpret and follow synchronicity's quiet whispers (*before* they become grunts, screams, or yells), the more you will find clarity in your life's purpose and radiate deep serenity, joy, and compassion from within. In resisting your intuition, life may become exceedingly difficult and even painful as Spirit finds another way to guide you to change.

It can be hard to process all the information that comes into your senses. In fact, if you were raised in Western culture, which promotes rationality above all other values (except perhaps irrational consumerism), you have likely muted or shut off your connection to nature altogether in order to fit into the culture, to get a job, and to hold everything together. This leaves people feeling disconnected from their inner nature and stretched between two opposing pulls.

In order to surmount the challenges we face, humanity's deepest potential for love and connection must awaken (and quickly) in the consciousness of every person on the planet—before we self-destruct. This process of self-destruction is evident in the bombing and poisoning of our planet, but what is less evident is that these external manifestations are an inherent product of our deeper psyches. We prefer to rally against the pain around us rather than face our own inner demons. It's time we stop blaming others for the suffering, pain, and loss in our lives and instead learn to tend our inner gardens and to manage the internal war zone in our minds and bodies—and, by extension, the environment, which is affected by our internal struggle. To experience beauty, peace, and love, we must start within.

Through our advancements in science, technology, and metaphysics, we are learning of the deep, essential interconnectedness of our hearts and minds. For so long, we've been trained to put ourselves into little boxes in order to fulfill the requirements of our education, our religious affiliation, our family status, and our work in the world. But now our economy, based on a capitalist, consumer-oriented lifestyle, is shattering, so many of us are finding ourselves disconnected and in pain from its destruction. If you are scrambling to keep it all together—or, similarly, other aspects of your life are in disruption and turmoil—perhaps you'll discover that those little boxes didn't fit you in the first place and the old pieces are not meant to come back together.

There is another way, beyond the boxes, and we need to awaken our deeper connection to Spirit in order to discover it. There is something new emerging.

Take a moment; look around. We are dealing with a society made sick by its own illnesses. Anxiety, fear, depression; obesity, grief, eating disorders; and bipolar tendencies, mental instability, and loss of vitality and purpose have become the new normal. Taking pharmaceutical drugs for these mental and emotional maladies has become our culture's new baseline. We are tortured by our efforts to try and fit into a society that does not acknowledge or respect our multi-dimensional natures and spiritual needs.

Beyond capitalism, corrupt politics, the corporatization of our society, and global fear tactics, there is a new era that is real—and it is waiting for you. When you learn to open yourself to the deep, multidimensional nature of reality, you will come to realize you live in a magical world where joy, love, and peace are in abundance. My hope is that by reading this book and using the simple keys I offer, you will meet me in that magical world—and perhaps even join me on my journey to stitch together a new society based on love, joy, connection, compassion, and . . . synchronicity.

Each one of us has a glitch within our psyche that needs our attention, a faulty program that was put there, either from our family inheritance, our societal programming, or the false beliefs we chose to adopt. It is imperative that we tend our mental garden and take note of the toxic thoughts that contaminate our minds and emotions. The things you judge or have strong feelings about are big clues to the areas of your mind that you need to explore and tend to. Taking time to write down the incessant thoughts, judgments, and limiting beliefs you have about yourself or others will help you uproot them. These thoughts hide in idle moments, like when you look in the mirror, or when you are waiting for someone, or before bed, or just after rising. What are your thought forms saying? Are they creating fertile soil or poisoning you?

Your thoughts are not true. They are not even yours; most likely, they are ideas you picked up from others. They work much like a virus being passed around unnoticed. By becoming aware of your thoughts, you can begin to dispel the ones that cause you pain and discomfort and choose other thoughts that are more positive and loving. Good thoughts will give you energy rather than consume energy.

Activate Your Star Seed

There is a star seed within you, planted by a divine hand; a potential for wondrous love that your mind can hardly fathom. This star seed has encoded within it the memory of your immortal nature, and contains within it the blueprint to your divine destiny.

Before arriving on this planet, you lived among the stars and understood your true nature. Then you descended here, by choice, to be animated in human form at this particular moment in time. There are no accidents. The day, time, and place of your birth, and the family to which you were born, were all selected to make up a set of challenges and teachings that you must acquire in order to live out your destiny.

Your star seed blueprint lives deep within you. When that seed is watered, nurtured, and cared for, you grow in its image. Your thoughts about your life are the soil in which it grows; your emotions, desires, relationships, and actions provide nutrients for your seed or they add toxins to the environment. As with any seed, just looking at it won't tell you how big and strong the plant will become; how you tend your inner garden (your unconscious and conscious thoughts) is what makes your star seed grow strong and hearty or causes it to wither and die.

The key to unlocking your star seed's potential lies within your heart's deepest desires. As with all seeds, your star seed needs to break open in order to sprout and take root. This is the hard part, the breaking apart of the old structure. But once the seed opens, it is no longer contained and can quickly begin to grow. While for some this is joyous, for many it is a painful yet miraculous experience. By following synchronicity and lovingly tending your inner garden now, when your potential is being tickled, you will be ready.

Your star seed does not contain the programming of your parents' wishes and dreams for you. It is not anything that your culture, society, or heritage has told you to become. Your star seed has a mysterious and magical unfolding that, if cared for in the right way, will grow into a beautiful, resilient, and powerful expression unique to you and you alone.

Your divine destiny will lead you to liberation and the deepest love imaginable. As your star seed grows and deepens its roots, you will eventually come to recognize that you are blooming among the fields of the New Earth—the inter-dimensional place where all those who have awakened to their deepest nature meet. The practices in this book will help you grow and bloom, in the here and now, exactly where your star seed is planted.

Flow in the River of Life

While our star seed must establish deep roots to grow into its fullest potential, our lives are meanwhile guided forward as if on a river, moving us from person to person and event to event. What is the nature and flow of this river, and why does it guide us as such?

When I am in the river of life, following the path of synchronicity, I feel carried, supported, and guided by an unseen hand. When synchronicity is absent, I am painfully aware that I have lost my way.

When you learn to flow with the natural rhythm of life, you will find yourself carried by an unseen river toward a beautiful destination. And as you learn to navigate even the fastest of white water rapids, in so doing, you will be able to recognize yourself as the true creator of your reality, and you will no longer be enslaved behind painful illusions. Are you ready to join me on this magical journey?

In the pages that follow, I will share with you how to attune more deeply to this river, how to awaken your star seed and align with your divine destiny.

Understand the Golden Thread That Connects Us

As we allow synchronicity to guide our lives, it weaves a golden thread that reconnects us to our humanity and awakens our dormant human potential. As you flow gracefully with the river, you awaken to the invisible threads of this golden latticework and anchor into the higher frequencies on the planet.

There is a frequency of divine grace and unconditional love, one that opens you to living into your ideals. By attuning to this frequency, you are reweaving this golden matrix of light and helping your star seed begin to take root. As you awaken this dormant potential, a new formation of light extends into the invisible space between you and others. This formation is the blossoming of our collective consciousness, and it ripples out across the planet in ways our minds have yet to comprehend.

When you are in the flow of synchronicity, feelings of trust, faith, surrender, love, and creativity abound. You are taking the path of least resistance, moving with the flow, and the river will carry you.

By following the Seven Keys in this book, you will be able to activate your potential to experience synchronicity in your life. There is a higher order to the way things work, one that is evident in the harmony of the natural world. Similarly, when you tune in to the rhythms, cycles, and seasons of your own life, a higher order of consciousness begins to awaken. You discover a knowing that arises from deep within yourself, and you become able to navigate your life with absolute clarity and focus. In addition, you will learn to surrender and release the need to control your life. In awakening to this deep knowing, you discover the true purpose for your life, beyond anything you studied in school or were told by outside sources.

As you will soon see, the Seven Keys are easy and do not require a lot of effort, though I do suggest daily practice. What is required most of all is a sincere heart and a dedication to seeking truth.

Are you ready to begin?

Follow the Path of Least Resistance

Synchronicity flows like a wave of energy and, as such, there is rhythm to it, a push and a pull, the negative and positive. Just like you can be carried by ocean tides moving in and out, you can ride the wave of synchronicity to flow toward your destiny.

Sometimes life will whisper softly and gracefully to move you in a different direction; at other times, it will hit you with a hardy slap in the face! I call these "course corrections," or, in the worst of circumstances, total "wipeouts." These can be a short and quick slap that just stings your cheeks a little, or a full-blown knock-out that leaves you down for the count. In either case, the course corrections or wipeouts happen to get you back on the wave and in flow. On such occasions, it is good to take time to check in with yourself and to release your resistance and your need to be in control, or else you may soon repeat the experience.

Like it or not, your life will course-correct to get you back on your divine path. When you are in deep resistance, ignoring the pain that's present in your life or pushing yourself too hard, you will face an inevitable course correction.

Why do we spend so much of our energy resisting our destiny? We get conditioned to ways of being that we have now outgrown or that are no longer good for us. Perhaps we are just doing what other people are doing, or what is considered normal. Most often, it is our hidden pain that keeps us trapped in old patterns. Eventually, we find that deep down, this patterning is not in line with our truest nature.

In July of 2015, the house I was living in with five others suddenly burned to the ground. Overnight, I lost my home, my personal belongings, and my home office. Perhaps worst of all, I lost my computer with all my years of writing and business plans, including my backups. In the morning, standing beside the smoldering ruins, all I had was the pajamas on my back and the shoes and jacket I hastily grabbed on my way out the door. Thank god no one was hurt in the fire. All six of us made it out just in time. There was no known cause for the fire and, unfortunately, I had let my renter's insurance lapse. But that's not the whole story.

With every darkness that has fallen upon my life, there has come a light. There is always a balance between the negative and the positive, the push and the pull. It is just the natural order of life, so I had faith things were going to be okay. Indeed, while I lost everything, the fire was nothing less than my wishes and dreams coming true!

Let me explain.

A mere two days before the fire, I hosted a closing ritual in my home with the recent students in a six-week Mystery School course, in which I was teaching many of the principles outlined in this book. This was our last gathering, so we finished the session with a prayer and a ceremonial release ritual. When it came time for me to say my prayer, I chose to let go of "stress and overwork," and I called in "sustainable new structures for growth."

The day after the workshop ended, I felt depleted. I needed a vacation like nobody's business. It had been exactly a year to the month that I had been living in this community house in Oakland, California. During that time, I had never taken more than a few days off to relax. However, just one year prior, I had been living in South India and happily referred to myself as a "Lady of Leisure." I did whatever aligned with my flow. But now, suddenly back in the Bay Area, in one of the most expensive cities in the world, I was eager to build my foundation and had fallen back into my old, ambitious ways of pushing myself. In the process, my ambition was overriding my innate wisdom, and no matter how hard I worked, I couldn't get above the hustle or back to my natural flow.

The day after I completed that ceremony with my students, I drove to my mom's house. She lives on the coast in a small beach town. Exhausted from the cycle I was in, I spent the entire one-hour drive crying. Before arriving at my mom's, I sat on the beach for a few hours to release my emotions and pray for guidance. The madness I had brought upon myself needed to stop.

By the time I got to my mom's house, I was even

more exhausted, depleted, and desperate for change. My brother generously took my mom and me out for a nice dinner. It was lovely to be with them. I became acutely aware of how disconnected I had become from my natural state by being in the insane hustle to make my life happen and to fit into my city surroundings. Pouring out my heart to my family over dinner, I shared with them how I couldn't live any longer with the lifestyle I had gotten myself into. I felt like I was killing myself trying to keep up with my monthly rent, and for what? To live in the city? I sensed that something had to change soon, but I had no idea how to change it. I wasn't ready to move back to India, and I had no idea where else to go.

After spending the night at my mom's, I felt a bit rejuvenated. Arriving back home late Monday afternoon, I started getting ready for another week of Oakland living. My new housemate, Rafael, and I had a short chat that afternoon, in passing. We both remarked how our lives had been guided by an unseen hand that had given us so many challenges to overcome in order to build resilience. As we shared our war stories of course corrections, we had a good laugh and felt relieved to find someone else understood. I shared how I had lost my father and spiritual teacher in July of 2003, and how in July of 2009 I had been robbed of my life's savings. July had somehow become a monumental month for me. She in turn shared her significant life transitions and synchronistic patterns. It was a deep conversation that moved us both to a place of awe and surrender to our lives, despite our big challenges.

Trying to go to sleep that night, I was relentlessly uncomfortable. I actually loved my house aesthetically and logistically, but for some reason, I became fixated on all the things I didn't like that about it. My room wasn't dark enough, and my nervous system couldn't relax. I needed more personal space. I wanted more trees, and a vegetable garden. I felt anxious and scared that my life force was shriveling up inside. With rents on the rise, I didn't feel like I could move, and I didn't know how to make a real change given my financial circumstances. I thought I needed to stick it out another year to get things on track. Push through it, I thought to myself. That's what people do in the city.

Perhaps things would be better if I changed the furniture in my room? Maybe that would give me a fresh perspective. I was trying to be resourceful and creative. Sitting on my bed, tossing and turning in discomfort, I pulled out my phone and started to surf Craigslist for new furniture. Just as I was sending an email request to make a bid for a beautiful new bed, I heard an explosion outside. I instantly jumped to my feet and instinctually threw my phone on my bed. Because it was not abnormal to hear gunshots or fireworks in our neighborhood, the rational part of me wanted to ignore it and go back to bed, but I couldn't. I needed to see if everyone was okay. I called out to Rafael thinking maybe her new bookshelf had fallen over. She came out of her room rubbing her eyes, not sure what was happening. I looked out the top floor window, and that's when I saw a fire bursting out of the windows on the first floor. Everyone else was still asleep.

I ran around the house screaming, "The house is on fire, get out now!" One by one, they came out of their rooms groggy-eyed and barely able to respond.

I was running up and down the stairs, trying to figure out who had misplaced the fire extinguisher, but the fire was too big, and the flames had already filled the first floor. Luckily, we all got out just in time; within ten minutes, the flames were through the roof and the building had been fully consumed.

Rafael and I stared at each other outside as we watched the house burn. "Really? We just talked about this earlier today!" We looked at each other in total amazement and wondered, once again, at the significance of these types of major "course corrections." Rafael had lived in the house for just two days. Even more incredibly, just two years prior to that, she had lost everything in a house fire. At least this time she had insurance.

It all seemed entirely familiar, yet all too tragic. The moment of grace was yet to come.

As I looked down at the t-shirt I was wearing, I was instantly full of wonder, amazement, and bliss— and I began laughing. At that moment, everything started to make sense, and I knew I was being set free. A euphoric feeling of ecstasy overcame me. It seemed so strange given what was happening, and it reminded me of the feeling I had when I watched my dad leave his body.

Just before going to bed, I felt an urge to wear a new t-shirt I had bought just a few weeks before at the

World One, Fourth of July festival. As the former head of a futuristic fashion magazine and fashion photographer, I am neither a person who ordinarily wears t-shirts nor someone who is inspired to buy clothes at festivals. In fact, I rarely shop for anything, so the purchase itself was unusual.

But the painting on this t-shirt had spoken to me from across the crowded outdoor music event, and I made a beeline toward it. It was the creation of a local artist and consisted of so many block prints layered one upon another that I wasn't sure what I was looking at. I instantly picked it up and bought it. My soul sister, Amanda, who was with me, and who knows my style really well, asked, "Really? Are you seriously going to wear that?" I had no idea why I liked the image on that shirt so much, but I could not stop staring at it. It was a red house with wings.

The day before at my mom's house, I had taken that shirt along. I had never even tried on the shirt, let alone worn it, but for some unexplainable reason, I hand-washed it, and then ironed it! Who irons t-shirts? It was a first for me. There was really no rhyme or reason to what I was doing. It felt as as if someone else were doing all of it through me.

Back home the next day, on the night of the fire, I took out that freshly washed and ironed t-shirt and tried it on for the first time, just before going to bed. I looked in the mirror, and I just laughed. I felt ridiculous. Why had I bought this t-shirt? It was not comfortable at all (especially to sleep in), and I just knew I would never wear it outside.

A few hours later, there I was, standing outside

in that crazy t-shirt and watching my house burn, and realizing this was now the only shirt I owned. I started laughing out loud at the embarrassment and thought of this being my only item of clothing left. This cosmic joke made me look down at the shirt, trying to come to terms with it being the only item I salvaged. That's when I realized the house painted on it looked eerily like an illustration of my own house that was burning before my eyes. The red paint looked like it was on fire, and the wings were carrying the house away (I've included a photo of the shirt here so you can see what I am describing). Behind the house is a green, block-print image of the Mother Mary on a throne with the baby Jesus on her lap, both of their crowns illuminated. On the back of the shirt, there are a lot of blue dogs and, on top of that, a skeleton dog who's reading a book with the moon above his head. The words "Dog-Eared Book" are printed under each dog. Each of the illustrations, symbols, and colors on the shirt had instant meaning to my soul. They began speaking to me at a level my mind could not totally comprehend. At that moment, I knew the entire drama was all part of a great design. I felt freed. I cried with joy and knew I was being completely guided and held through that extreme experience.

Before the fire, I was unwilling to make changes and felt unable to slow down, even though I knew I needed to. The house fire was a massive course correction and an act of divine grace. That shirt I purchased on a whim finally made sense. It was time to let go and, once again, allow Spirit to guide me. A serious course correction had been made, and I was listening.

A few months after the fire, I moved to a cabin in a pristine setting among ancient redwoods, an hour away from the nearest grocery store or gas station. It was a paradise for me and provided deep healing. In the next section, Key #2, I'll share how the magic of synchronicity guided me there.

Key #2
Get Honest with Yourself

"The root cause of the whole misery of life is lack of awareness." – Patanjali

Aligning with synchronicity requires radical truth telling. This doesn't mean you need to go and shout your truth from the rooftops, or even tell your closest allies. This is really about getting radically honest with yourself.

Are you sweeping things under the carpet? Are you ignoring serious pain points in your life, hoping they will resolve on their own? Is there a part of your life in which you are chronically unhappy?

Getting radically honest is more difficult than it even sounds. It's about admitting to yourself things you know will require change. When you become clear that something is not right or is amiss in your life, magic can happen very quickly—sometimes instantly. The truth of your situation becomes a glaring reality once it's acknowledged. At such times, it may get so bad that you will *have to* make a change. If you don't, by another seeming twist of fate, it will change for you.

In order to avoid massive course corrections, such as your house burning down or contracting a debilitating disease, it's important that you learn to course-correct on your own and by your own free will. This isn't always easy or possible, but it's good to keep in mind. This can be the hardest choice you make. It might require you to leave a toxic relationship, to step away from an unhealthy workplace, or—as in my case——to move to a healthier environment or find another resourceful solution.

The good news is that the truth really does set you free. It may sting at first. It may cause you a lot of sleepless nights. It may disturb something that has become settled. But ultimately, it will liberate you.

A wise man in India once told me, "Tell the truth intelligently." Those words were medicine for me on my journey of radical truth telling. I wasn't always the most intelligent truth-teller. I'd been told I could be blunt and harsh with my desire to share my truth. Over the years, I have learned to tell the truth more intelligently and to seek grace in my desire to live an authentic life.

When you are closed, fixed, and shut down in denial, you block the flow that is destined for you and wanting to express through you; you block synchronicity and the flow of healthy nutrients to your seed. Such blocks often feel like a pressure-filled hosepipe that is kinked. Eventually, the pipe will burst, and, all too often, you will find that happening in drastic ways, like disease, accidents, or heartbreak.

With truth, on the other hand, come new opportunities and new choices. When you are honest with yourself and those around you, you open the path to healing and transformation. Only then do radical, new, and potent fields of possibility present themselves. Only then do you get to see what you are made of and explore your true potential. Only then does the star seed awaken to take root, grow, and eventually flower.

Many people are afraid of what will happen if they get too honest—like when bad habits take hold, the mind freaks out, or your relationships need to adjust. This is all cause for fear to build up in your system, and fear blocks the flow of synchronicity and your ability to read the signs.

Self-denial is tricky; it hides in the subconscious mind. But the more you practice honesty, the easier it becomes to spot the clever little games you play with yourself. You know, the ones that keep you stuck and playing the victim.

The more you practice radical honesty with yourself, the sooner your life transforms into beauty, becomes filled with your ideals, and unfolds along the path of your divine destiny. Being honest with yourself isn't always easy, but it's vital.

Identify Where You Are Stuck

Why do you hold on to what is familiar? Are you afraid of what might be if you let go? I know I am not the only one who does this, as I see it happening all around me. We often live in denial, grasping toward the familiar, failing to embrace what is imminent, and not seeing the promise of what lies ahead if we simply let go and allow things to change. When things are meant for us, they come back again and again. We don't need to grasp or cling.

Change is inevitable. You can try to hold tight and ensure some sense of security and consistency, but it won't make things stay the same. Change is a natural part of life's unfolding; it is programmed into our biology. In an ideal world, you would accept change and welcome your new life. The trick is how to move through change gracefully, how to allow it to bring in fresh air, new ideas, and new ways of being.

I observe this dynamic most often in relationships. People are so afraid of losing what they perceive as security and comfort, regardless of how unhappy they may be together. We simply do not like to navigate change when it arises. It's uncomfortable and awkward, and it just plain sucks. But there is an inherent problem in not accepting or allowing things or people to change. When you become rigid and fixed, complacent and stubborn, you are saying "No" to your own evolution. You are saying "No" to the flourishing of your own soul.

To be carried in the river of synchronicity, you have to be willing to change. You have to face your fears in the mirror and smoke out the little demons that play tricks in your mind. Any part of you that is unwilling to change, any part of you that is grasping and holding—that is what you will need to look at. That is what you need to address. I promise you it is not as scary as it sounds. It's worth it, because, as I am sure you have yourself heard, whatever we resist will persist.

Take a moment to get honest with yourself right now. Grab your journal and write down answers to the following questions:

- What are you afraid of?
- What part of your life is stuck or not flowing?
- What are you willing or unwilling to let go of? Be specific.

For help getting clear about where you are blocked, unhappy, or fearful, download my worksheet, "How Balanced Is Your Life?" (KnowTheSelf.com/workbook). It will guide you through a simple exercise to identify where you are not satisfied by looking at eight areas of your life: love, health, spirituality, life purpose, finances, leisure, friends, and family. This is a great tool to use anytime you feel confused, stuck, stressed out, or bored with your life.

As I've said before, even by simply identifying where in your life you are stuck or fearful, magical things may begin to happen. You will enter into the flow of synchronicity. When you become honest about something in your life that needs to change, golden doorways will open. This always surprises people. I can't count the number of calls I routinely receive from my clients and friends, sharing with me synchronistic events with a sense of awe and wonder. It is exciting when things seem to magically align in life, but it is not eerie or unexplainable. It often happens when we begin to get honest with ourselves about where we are stuck and open ourselves to the flow.

Understand the Law of Rhythm

By now, I imagine you've heard of The Law of Attraction. This law states that you literally create your reality through the way your thoughts, feelings, words, and actions send signals, as vibrations, out into your environment. Whatever you put out in the world comes back to you. People often use this principle to attract more of what they want in life. It is a powerful law to understand because it empowers you to create your life consciously.

There are other Universal Laws by which we are governed. One is The Law of Rhythm. This law states that everything moves and vibrates in a rhythm or frequency. These rhythms establish the seasons, cycles, stages of development, and patterns in your life. When you attune to synchronicity and the path of least resistance, you begin to flow with the cycles of life toward your divine destiny, and magical doorways and opportunities become a daily occurrence. Life begins to flower and unfold in a beautiful new direction.

As you come to experience and understand how the universe organizes itself, synchronistic moments will become your breadcrumbs of hope and your confirmation that you are on your path.

In the workbook, you will find a list of the Universal Laws that govern our lives, you can download one here: KnowTheSelf.com/workbook.

* * *

After my house fire, it was clear to me that Spirit was rearranging my life for the better as an answer to my prayers. Moment to moment, I felt as if I were surfing a tsunami of synchronicity as things magically aligned. Even though I only had $1,000 in the bank, I didn't have any insurance, and I had just lost everything I owned, I knew without a single doubt that I was being guided to a higher order of cosmic orchestration.

Everything I needed after the fire was gifted to me. A huge pile of clothes, all in my size, came to me, and multiple people started recovery funds in my name. I was welcomed with open arms everywhere I landed. This was a feeling I had always longed for, and though it came by a drastic measure, it also taught me important experiential lessons. For a stubborn, self-sufficient person who has a hard time asking for help, it was truly humbling and awe-inspiring to learn how to receive from others.

Prior to the fire, my pattern had been only to trust in my own ability to fill my needs. I carried a lot of grief in my heart from the lack of support I felt for most of my life. I was unable to see what I actually had around me. I tend to put my mission in life ahead of my needs for trust and deep connection, so I believe I was somehow holding at bay the support that was trying to find me. Unconsciously, I hoped that by focusing on my mission in service to others that my own needs would magically be met without my having to voice them, but it wasn't happening, and I needed to be absolutely shocked and in desperate need in order to ask for and receive the support I had always longed for. Ugh, a bit dramatic, but now I know to ask for help sooner.

* * *

A few weeks after the fire, as the shock started wearing off, I got a call from my dear friend Allison who sensed I needed a helping hand. She invited me to her beautiful property high up on the ridge near Point Reyes, just north of San Francisco. Her phone call was a godsend! What I needed more than anything was to get out of the city and relax in nature, but I had been too shell-shocked to take any action.

On the drive to Allison's house, I had my first cry since the fire. Once it started, I couldn't turn it off. My two-hour drive was filled with tears, and I even pulled over to call my mom and cried to her for an hour, but still the tears wouldn't turn off. When I arrived at Allison's house I tried to keep my composure, but it wasn't possible. We sat down in the kitchen and she patiently listened to my frustration and sadness. I was exhausted from having looked at so many apartments and rooms for rent, and finding nothing suitable. I felt homeless and broken. Allison was clearly uncomfortable seeing me cry, and meanwhile, her husband had gotten up and began pacing around behind me somewhere. In all the 16 years I'd known Allison, that was probably the only time she'd seen me that emotional.

Thank god for good friends!

Allison listened patiently for a few minutes before she realized this was absurd behavior for me. She really didn't miss a beat. "Hey, come on. This isn't like you. You don't use Craigslist to find homes! Surely your next home will come from your personal network. What are you looking for? What do you want?"

Her words sounded like magic to my ears. "What do I want?" I sat up and looked her right in the eye. "I want a cabin in the woods so I can write my book." Ahh, just saying that out loud made me instantly stop crying. At that exact moment, her husband appeared from wherever he had been waiting out the storm of my emotions and said, to my great surprise and delight, "I have a cabin in the woods. No one is living there. You can stay there for a while."

Stranger yet, I then received a random text message from my dear friend (and fellow seer) Barry a few minutes later that read, "I have one thing to say to you, Mendocino County." While it turns out that Barry and his partner have been eyeing potential retirement properties there for years (unbeknownst to me), Barry and I had not spoken in days and the content and timing of his message was a complete shock to us all. As it turned out, the cabin I had just moments earlier found out I could move into was, in fact, located in Mendocino County. And it continued, now rather eerily, with Barry's next message: "Don't tell me it's on 'xxx' street?" In fact, it was on that very same street!

And so it goes with magical doorways.

* * *

If you want to live in synchronicity, you simply need to be honest with yourself and learn how to interpret the signs and symbols. Riding the wave of synchronicity feels like taking a magical carpet ride. Some people think that following synchronicity is a silly pastime or only for ungrounded people who are flitting about and poring over superstitious omens. It can look like that from the outside looking in, but for the one who is experiencing the synchronicity, it is pure wonder and a connection to the unseen orchestration that governs life.

It doesn't matter what other people think. Synchronicity is a sacred connection to the divine, yet it is also a personal experience that very few people can share with you. It is your deepest nature animating and reflecting itself back to you. **It is magic made manifest.**

Synchronicity happens in the small conversations between your heart and the unseen hand that guides you. And it is shaped by your conversations with the natural world.

When you practice the steps outlined in this book, you will experience for yourself what it feels like to walk down your own golden brick road that leads you home.

Decode Signs and Symbols

What many people get tripped up about in following synchronicity is, what do all these hair-raising, goosebump-causing situations mean?

Sometimes, synchronicity speaks through dreams. As I was writing this book, a telephone repairman named Brian came to my house and shared his story with me. Brian dreamt of an old man watching a Western movie on TV. In another room, he saw model airplanes hanging from the ceiling, relics of World War

II. He woke up the next day and when he arrived at his job site and entered the customer's home, he saw the same old man from his dream, watching a Western movie on TV, and in another room, he saw model airplanes from World War II hanging from the ceiling! He got a bit spooked and chalked it up to déjà vu.

In Brian's case, I would call his experience a dream premonition or a past-life connection. Perhaps that man and Brian had something important to discuss about WWII. Or perhaps it was Spirit's way of letting Brian know he has a gift of premonition. He could practice to see if he can rely on it; before he goes to sleep, he can specifically ask for another premonition dream and track its accuracy.

Synchronistic messages are fun to get curious about. You can be your own private detective solving your own life's mystery.

When a synchronicity like the one Brian experienced appears in your life, it is time to slow down and listen with your other senses. Track and record your experiences. You will find that, over time, common themes are trying to get your attention. There will be various ways to translate the synchronistic messages you receive. Play around with them to find what makes sense to you. Not all synchronicities mean, "yes" or are good. Some people tell me because it was a synchronicity they assumed it meant it was a green light for what they were asking about. This is not always the case. Synchronistic events show us how the Universe communicates with us; it is up to us to determine the meaning. The synchronicity itself is simply showing you the interconnectedness of all things, but how you interpret the meaning is totally dependent on you and what you make things mean.

All of life will begin to speak with you through the natural world and through symbols, including animals, plants, the weather, the cosmos, numbers, and signposts. All that is alive (animate and inanimate) will begin to commune with your frequency. You will become in tune with the natural world when you tune in to your original nature and discover your true essence. Tribal people and those who live close to the earth understand this deep connection. There is a harmony between all things.

Spirit communicates in metaphors, and it is rarely ever direct. This often causes frustration, but I like to view it more as an investigation. There are a great many resources online and in ancient texts that can help you decode the language of Spirit. Some example keyword searches you can try online when you want to decode your messages might include: dream interpretation, numerology, astrology, animal totem medicine, color interpretation, sacred geometry, music theory, quantum physics, and spiritual science. Those are all great avenues for exploring; they can help give meaning to your clues. You could also try divination techniques, like using pendulums, tarot cards, I Ching, runes, numerology, and oracle cards.

However, the simplest and most important way to understand and decode your synchronistic events is to figure out what you are feeling when signs reveal themselves and tune in to what the symbols mean to you. It can get really confusing and twisted up if you rely too heavily on outside sources. So be curious and allow yourself to do free association.

When you allow your mind to be in an open state, you will suddenly find you can understand things without trying to cognize them at all. The answer will just magically click in your head, and you will know what those synchronistic symbols are directing you toward.

Remember that your path is your path. No one can walk it for you, and no one can tell you what your synchronicity experiences mean. Some skilled spirit communicators can help you decode them, but you will still need to check in with your own inner wisdom to see if their explanations resonate with you. Do not take on other people's interpretations or fears if they don't make sense to you.

Learning to trust your intuition is the number one goal for being in the flow. This inner way of knowing—using your gut sense—will direct your path. Your mind, however, will confuse you at every turn. Your mind will get twisted up and hyper-activated when synchronicity speeds up and events become more bizarre. These are moments to get really quiet and go inward. If you find yourself becoming paranoid or looking up every symbol you find, take a break and sit in meditation.

Your intuition and open heart are your biggest assets, and your breath is your most trusted guide. Stick to focusing on your breath and your inner knowing, and I assure you it will all be figured out in due time.

Something to check when you react to an exciting synchronic event is how you feel. What is your initial response before you translate the event with your mind? Do you have a fight-or-flight impulse? Do you feel a warning? Are you smiling? Are you nervous? These are good indications that can help you notice what is alive inside of you.

This is where people often get tripped up. If you feel fear in reaction to signs, it is important to sit still, pray, and face the fear inside a meditative state until you can see through it. Reacting from a place of fear will only make you suffer. The sooner you can face your fears and move through them, the swifter flow will move you toward your divine destiny.

* * *

No one taught me how to follow synchronicity. At the age of 17, I left home to travel and learn about the world. When I looked at what was being offered in college, it felt stifling and controlling. It wasn't for me. I set out to travel in foreign lands and follow signs. I felt that if there was, indeed, a divine plan for my life, the signs would lead me to it. It was just a knowing I had. What I was seeking was the truth behind the madness; unconditional love, kindness, and a place where I would fit in. It was my simple prayers that led me to discover the magic of synchronicity and flowing with the river of life. When I would pray in earnest and focus with all my heart, my prayers were always answered, one hundred percent of the time!

Knowing how to pray with my heart started at a very early age. When I was five years old and my sister, eight, we shared a bedroom. We would pray out loud together every night before we went to bed. Those innocent prayers always started out with asking each other for forgiveness for all the mean things we had done to each other that day. After we forgave each other, we would share what we were grateful for. Then we would ask God, with all our hearts, for the things we wanted most. Sometimes they were sweet, sincere things we wanted, like, "May everyone be happy." At other times, they were selfish desires for a new doll or whatever we wanted our parents to buy for us.

One particular night, my sister prayed for a black stallion. She loved horses; she was kind of obsessed with them. She desperately wanted to have her own horse. When she prayed out loud, I would pray with her inside my head. That evening, my sister and I both imagined how amazing it would be if she had her very own horse. We both went to sleep dreaming about it. I was convinced our parents would buy her a horse because I could see it so clearly, as if it had already happened. Before we fell asleep, I assured my sister they would get her one.

The next morning, I woke up before she did and went downstairs to see if anyone else was awake. Whenever I was the first one to wake up, I had a habit of sitting on the couch in the living room in front of the big picture window. As I sat there, patiently waiting for everyone else to wake up, I looked out front to where my sister and I played every day. We had a wide, three-foot-high retaining wall made of stone on our front porch. We loved pretending that the wall was our horse. We would practice riding there. We'd strap our jump ropes over our feet, using the plastic handles as stirrups and the rope as reins, and happily tap our feet against the stone wall to make the sound of horse hooves on pavement, saying "Giddy-up, horsey." It was a favorite game of ours.

That morning, as I sat on the living room couch staring out the window, I got the shock of my five-year-old life. Right there beside our horsey wall stood a great white horse! It was real, it was alive, and it didn't have a bridle or saddle. It looked like it had been plucked from horse heaven and placed on our front doorstep. God had manifested my sister a horse; it was the wrong color, but it was real. And I would get to ride it, too!

I ran upstairs and shook my sister awake. "The horse—it's here!" She didn't believe me, but we had a sliding glass door and balcony just off our bedroom, and I flung it open so she could look underneath our window and see it with her own eyes. I will never forget the look in her eyes. It was the happiest I had ever seen her.

We began squealing with absolute delight, and an overwhelming sense of divine orchestration awoke within me. God really does answer prayers! My mom was beside herself trying to calm us down. She explained as kindly (and firmly) as she could that it was not our horse, that she had not bought it, that we could not keep it, that it was not an early Christmas present, and that we needed to let go of such ideas.

A few phone calls later, we learned that the horse belonged to the stable down the road and had somehow escaped. When the rightful owner came to collect the mysteriously freed horse, my sister fell on the ground in a pool of tears. I sat dumbfounded on the couch in absolute awe, amazement, and wonder. For me, even though it wasn't going to be our horse, I'd received all the assurance I needed to know that when I truly wanted something from deep in my heart, it would be provided. It took me another 20 years to realize that manifesting selfish desires brings pain and suffering; I still had some growing up to do.

If you have never experienced an answer to a prayer, or experienced synchronistic, miraculous events, you are simply not seeking deeply enough. I learned this great lesson by buying a one-way ticket to a foreign country where I knew absolutely no one, didn't speak the language, and had only $100 to my name; and somehow, I survived for six months.

If you allow yourself to be guided, without a destination in mind but with a longing in your heart, your prayers will open doors. When you strip off the security you have clung to, you begin to realize there is something much grander holding you in place. When you learn to lean into that knowing, you will find that magic is all around you. I promise.

Find the Rhythm of Your Soul

When you are in the flow of synchronicity, you needn't worry; you are being guided, and you are free to relax. Your pushing and striving will step aside, and you can to settle into your heart. By connecting deeply to yourself and to your own internal rhythm, you will be able to tune into the rhythm of your soul.

We each have a unique rhythm. When you find the rhythm of your soul, your path will be illuminated.

It is imperative to stabilize yourself according to your own rhythm. No one can do this for you. It does not come from the outside.

By tuning to your inner rhythm every day, you will find your life opening up in extraordinary ways. You might find you came here to do something that truly frightens you or pushes you beyond what you thought was possible for yourself. This is normally the first realization that you are actually tuning in to your divine destiny.

Here's something to try. Become quiet within yourself. Close your eyes. Can you hear the rhythm of the airways? That question might sound strange at first, but see if you can pick up a tune, if only for a moment. Allow your voice to carry that tune. This isn't a song you have heard before; it will be a new song, fresh every time. There is no need to try and grab it, or remember it—however beautiful it may sound. It is simply for living in the present moment and using it to help you attune to the rhythm of your life.

Try to do this while you are driving, or walking on a trail alone. Look to the heavens and see if you can hear a tune. There's no need to force it or push toward it. It simply comes when you relax into it. Soften your mind. Start making a small sound, a hum. Allow your mouth to take new shapes while allowing your throat to open. You may hear the voice of angels. You may hear a lullaby. You may hear your ancestors' voices. You may hear the Earth, or nature spirits. Allow yourself to commune with the rhythm of nature in this way.

By tuning your vocal chords to flow, to the vibration of the airways, you give voice to the field of possibility. If you aren't hearing anything, begin to tone with vowel sounds: ah–ee–oh–uhm–ahm–aum. These sounds can get you going and open the channels of frequency that live inside you.

This is not a performance. This is not for anyone else to experience. This song is only for you. Once the vibration begins to move through you, it will awaken in you a sleeping memory of sweetness.

If you don't like your voice, or feel that you sing off-key, don't worry. The more you practice, the more you will find your own rhythm, your own harmony. The sounds you make will start to harmonize with your inner frequency.

You can sing in your head to yourself if you are at work or around people you don't want listening. Just keep a tune alive inside yourself and you will find your flow, your own personal rhythm. If you are a musician or want to take this feeling to the next level, begin hosting or going to jam sessions. Improvisational music allows you to find tunes from the airwaves and vocalize them. It is really fun to play them out on a percussion instrument with others.

When you are able to find a rhythm, it helps you find the pace at which the river of life is carrying you. Some days, the river will be calm and slow; some days it will be faster. If you are an improvisational musician, you know this feeling of tuning in to a natural rhythm really well. But even if you have never picked up an instrument, you can attune to this flow with your voice or with simple percussion sounds like tapping your foot, clapping your hands, or playing drum sounds on a table with your hands and fingers.

You might find it easier to dance to the airwaves. Close your eyes and allow yourself to sway side to side, allow yourself to flow and you just might find yourself doing improvisational dance, or some type of body-based stretching to an invisible sound.

This can feel totally weird at first, so I highly suggest doing it when you are alone and only when you feel safe in your place of comfort. If singing out loud or moving your body in tune with this internal rhythm does not feel comfortable to you, you can always practice all of this inside your imagination. That can also have a wonderful effect.

Play with tuning in to your own personal frequency and see what happens. All it takes to play with the rhythm of your soul is a willing heart, a smile, and knowing that there is no way to fail. Give it a try. When you do this often, or before meditation, it will deepen your connection to flow. Your senses will expand and the vibration will clear your channels. It will bring you joy, sweetness, and relief. Give it a try. Email me and let me know how it works for you: info@KnowTheSelf.com.

Key #3
Slow Down to Speed Up

"We are not at peace with others because we are not at peace with ourselves, and we are not at peace with ourselves because we are not at peace with God."
— Thomas Merton

It is so common to look outside ourselves for answers. We often talk with our friends and family about our problems. We even share our problems online, asking our "friends" on Facebook for ideas about how to proceed with the challenges and issues we face.

We constantly seek outside ourselves to find our way. To some extent, this is normal; it's how we interact and share our lives with others. But there comes a time in life when looking outside doesn't work anymore. You will know when this happens because the advice people give you won't add up to your own internal knowing of what's right and wrong for you. At these times, it's imperative that you listen to your own inner guidance. This is when it's time to seriously slow down and listen in.

There is a simple practice of tuning within that I want to share with you. There are three points of focus that will enable you to hear your inner voice. When you stop and listen to your inner wisdom, you can move forward much more swiftly and with grace and ease, rather than crawling or clawing your way forward. Often, if you slow down or stop, you'll find a quantum leap ahead of you that will catapult you effortlessly in a bright new direction.

The meditation practice I am about to share allows you to know yourself as a "vertical axis being" who is having a horizontal experience. I'll unpack that statement so you really understand what I mean and why it's important that we remember our vertical axis nature. Before you roll your eyes and check out, I want you to wait a moment. Stay with me here, because this is a key to unlocking the inner doorway to your true nature and opening yourself to synchronicity.

First, I'll explain your basic human energetic anatomy. You have a field of energy around your body that is constantly interacting with your environment and everyone you come into contact with. This energetic field exists, even if you can't see it or feel it. It has been measured by electromagnetic devices and is called a torus field pattern. It is shaped like an orb of energy around you with openings at the top and bottom that pull in energy from above and below. Your body stands in the central channel.

This is a torus field pattern from the top view looking down:

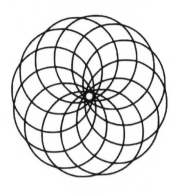

This toric field vortex is the energetic pattern of your field. Imagine this image shown above as a beautiful latticework of light particles above your head spinning like a portal. Allow it to drop over your head like a hat, placing your head at that central point. Allow this beautiful, spinning shape to move down and around you so you are standing in the center of an orb of light with this pattern rotating all around you. Your head will be popping out of the central column, and your feet popping out at the bottom of this cylinder-shaped field.

The field of energy around your body is called your "morphogenetic field." Physicists around the world are finally discovering the mysterious nature of this field that yogis, mystics, Egyptians, Incans, Mayans, and indigenous people around the world have known about for thousands of years. If you want a scientific understanding of the morphogenetic field, I recommend reading Lynne McTaggart's book *The Field* or checking out Rupert Sheldrake's work on morphic resonance.

The morphogenetic field around your body sends and receives energy. It is made of light particles and information highways. In Sanskrit texts, these energy channels are referred to as "nadis," and they flow light through to your major energy centers along your spine. There are 350,000 nadis charted in the ancient yogic text, Shiva Samhita.

You can feel into your own morphogenetic field through your intuitive senses. Simply by using your intention and focus, you can begin to tune your field to a higher frequency in order to sync up with the river of life and your divine destiny. When you are running negative patterns, your field gets distorted. It is important to keep your nadis clear and your field full of light, with all the channels on. All living creatures have this field of light around their bodies.

In order to flow in the river of life toward your divine destiny, you need to align with nature—your inner nature—and mimic the natural world, which is already in perfect harmony. Look to the mountains, forests, and valleys. Spend time near bodies of water. Get close to animals. Using their example, take responsibility for your life and what you create around yourself. This means going beyond blaming people or circumstances for your situation and taking responsibility for your part of the drama. This can be a really hard thing to do. No more pity parties!

Most of us go through life emoting and expressing ourselves, often without a clue as to how we affect other people or how our energy is affecting those around us—even when we are not talking. You know the feeling you get when you find yourself drained by certain people and you don't know why? You might find yourself avoiding them, or needing to take a nap after speaking to them. Or you might not even realize that you tend to drain other people and you don't know why they are avoiding you. You know what I am talking about. This happens to all of us.

In order to experience true liberation and inner peace, we need to learn how to source our energy from the vertical plane, rather than the horizontal. The horizontal plane is where the push/pull dynamic lives. This is the dynamic that you get into with people when you try to source your pleasure from them or blame them for your pain. This is also the plane of resistance and struggle. This is a very tricky dynamic to unwind, as we are all habituated to this horizontal plane of existence. You may have become conditioned to blaming others for your sad stories and expecting others to make you happy. You may blame your environment and often find yourself stressed and struggling through life.

There is a wonderful way of stopping this interplay between the push/pull dynamic that you get trapped in, that we all get trapped in. What you need to do is remember you are a vertical-axis being having a horizontal experience and tune to the vertical plane.

When you understand that you are a spiritual being connected through space and time to all that is, you can see the physical dimension is just a horizontal drama.

In the physical, horizontal plane, you participate in pleasure and pain, right and wrong, good and bad. You are fixated on the past and the future. But when you let go of the black and white and shift to the vertical, you experience freedom. You experience present time.

When you operate from your vertical axis, you don't need possessions to make you happy; you no longer need people to make you happy. You can actually tune yourself to liberation, salvation, understanding, pure love, forgiveness, and bliss. You open up to your true self and find that it is clear, honest, and ever-present in your life. All you need to do is to tap into your vertical nature and tune yourself to this higher state of being. When you do this, flow happens naturally. There is nothing to force, and your life comes into alignment.

You actually need to slow down to speed up. Sitting still is not something you cognize; it is something you actualize. It happens in your body. You can't simply think about it. This practice of slowing down to speed up is non-negotiable. You have to do it to understand it. Stilling the mind, slowing the breath, and stopping all activity is imperative to catching the river of life. The practice I am about to share with you will teach you how.

Ground Out

Before you start a meditation practice or whenever you are feeling spaced out, it is time to "ground out." "Grounding" is a word I heard a lot in New Age lingo scenes. When I first heard someone tell me, "You need to ground out," I thought that meant go outside and put my bare feet in the dirt. That morphed into imagining an umbilical cord dropping out of the base of my spine and growing roots into the earth.

While both of those versions of grounding can be helpful, what I learned from a wise Native American elder has proven much more effective for the type of explosive energy that I carry. If you are dealing with a kundalini awakening, severe anxiety, or have experienced heightened states of trauma in your body, this is the type of grounding to practice because it will keep you safe and present in your body, rather than dissociating or astral traveling.

Since your body is primarily made of water, you are an electrical conductor of energy. When dealing with high vibrational frequencies and unlocking your star seed gifts, it is imperative to ensure your body is grounded to the Earth and you are "embodied."

By living in modern cities and high-tech homes, we are bombarded by electromagnetic fields, and our bodies often lose connection with the Earth. We no longer sleep on bare earth; we cover our feet, we pave our roads and pathways, and some of us live in high-rises. All of these conditions detach us from the Earth, and we need to consciously stay connected in order to heal ourselves and hold our awakened senses comfortably in our bodies.

Grounding

In order to consciously awaken the authentic Self we need to be present in our bodies. Too often, we leave our body by disassociating, afraid of intense feelings. To restore our personal power, and understand our life purpose, we need to become comfortable with bodily sensations and treat the physical vehicle as a temple of divine consciousness.

The first step is learning how to Ground...

1. Imagine the **crystal core** at the center of the Earth. This is the heart of the Earth/Mother.

2. Imagine a **beam of energy connecting** you to the crystal core. Use any imagery that helps you connect - like a tree trunk or a beam of light. Make sure this connection to the Earth stays wider than your body.

3. Allow the energy of the **Earth to move up through your feet** and into your entire body, all the way above your head. You may notice different colors or sensations in your body as you make this connection stronger. By connecting to the center of the Earth you can de-stress and ground-out any excess energy.

4. Allow the energy of the Earth to **pool and collect in your heart** to awaken your true nature.

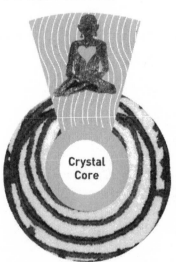

Crystal Core

Benefits

∞ Restore your internal balance.

∞ Hold firm & steady in your body.

∞ Release excess energy.

∞ Become present in the here and now.

∞ Understand your feelings.

The Earth is our Mother, unconditionally loving, holding us tightly through her magnetic gravitational field. She gives us nourishment, support, and composts all our pain into fertile soil. Respect her. Protect her. She is our home.

Grounding only takes a few minutes to practice, and it only takes practicing this successfully for a period of time to master. After repetitive conditioning, your grounding will become a constant and sustainable force and will aid your life greatly.

Please make sure you are doing this grounding exercise before and after you meditate and throughout the day—whenever you feel your energy or anxiety rise. This is the first step in creating your Vertical Alignment.

Before attempting it, take a look at the diagram to better understand what grounding might look like in your imagination. You can download this diagram along with the entire Companion Workbook online: KnowTheSelf.com/workbook.

Establish Vertical Alignment

Make sure you are in a safe, quiet, and private place to do this exercise of establishing Vertical Alignment. Ideally, create a recharge station in your home where you can commit to doing this simple exercise on a daily basis. Having a small altar in the place where you recharge will help designate it as a sacred place, and the more you sit there, the more the energy will build up.

This recharge station could be in the corner of a room or even in a closet—anywhere you feel safe and will not be disturbed. For some people, the only place they feel they have privacy is in their car. If that is your case, do the best you can with what you have, and do this exercise in your parked car. Or you can go outside (weather permitting) and find a place in your garden or in a nearby park and try it there.

Having a personal recharge station and altar is not necessary, but it can make your practice stronger and it allows you to go deeper faster. But you can do this practice on a crowded subway and still be successful in connecting to the flow.

Personally, I like to light a candle and a stick of incense and have sacred symbols of meaning in front of me to help me deepen my experience and to keep me in a state of spiritual awareness.

Have your journal next to you so that after your experience, you can jot down any insights you gained.

To be guided through this exercise, you can download my Eleven-Minute Vertical Alignment Meditation along with the workbook: KnowTheSelf.com/workbook.

How to establish Vertical Alignment:

1. Find a quiet and safe space, close your eyes, and begin by taking three to ten deep, clearing breaths to quiet your mind and relax your body. Take as many conscious, deep breaths as it takes to get quiet inside.

2. With your mind's eye, draw a perfect circle around your body at least three feet out and all around you. Ask that any energy that is not yours (that you picked up from the outside or grabbed from someone else) be removed from this circle. This is your

personal space. Stay here until you feel clear. Transform your circle into a three-dimensional orb around your body.

3. Imagine the iron crystal core of the Earth. This core is within the molten lava, in the heart of the Earth; this is the intelligence of the Earth.

4. Imagine a beam of energy connecting the heart of the Earth, the crystal core, to your heart. Make sure this beam of energy (also known as a cord) is wider than your body and fills your personal space. Allow the energy of the Earth to move up through your feet and into your entire body, all the way above your head, grounding your entire orb. Allow the Earth energy to pool and collect in your heart. Take as many breaths as needed to feel the impact this connection to the Earth creates in your body. You might notice your body feeling heavier, more relaxed. Your breath will deepen and your mind will soften. Pause until you feel sure of the connection.

5. Imagine the Central Sun, which is in the center of our galaxy, beyond our solar sun. It holds our galaxy in order. Pouring out from the Central Sun, imagine a beam of energy gently reaching down to you, like liquid light, into the top of your head and filling your body, mixing and merging with the energy of the Earth—pooling together in your heart. Hold this awareness as long as possible.

Allow this energy to circulate through your body, cleansing and clearing all your electrical channels. Allow this energy to illuminate your body, tissues, muscles, and blood. It will feel soothing and will increase your capacity for healing any ailments.

6. Stay as long as you can in this Vertical Alignment, with your awareness held at your heart center. Pay attention to any feelings that arise. Allow your mind to wander—as long as you stay connected to your breath. If you wander too far out of your body, use your breath as your guide to come back to the feeling of being centered in your heart. Feel into your being-ness, that sense of being you, exactly as you are, a soul having a human experience.

Whenever you practice Vertical Alignment, give yourself plenty of time to listen deeply. Once you have established the connection with the Earth's heart and the Central Sun, you become an open channel to your true dimensional essence. Wonderful things happen in the silence once the alignment is activated.

Journal about your experiences. Your heart center is the place of communion between the spiritual and physical worlds. It is a portal and a gateway to a beautiful multi-verse. The longer you can keep your awareness focused in your heart, the faster you will align with your divine destiny. You can refer to the diagram below, or online here for more about this exercise, Slowing Down to Speed Up: KnowTheSelf.com/workbook.

Vertical Alignment

Connect to your Authentic Self in Present time.

The Central Sun : Beyond our Sun, there is one brighter, housed in the Pleiadian star system. This Sun is the center of our Galaxy and is the source of life. We restore our internal balance by connecting to it consciously.

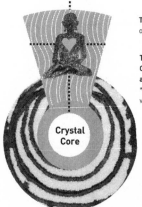

Crystal Core

The Horizontal Plane is our 3D reality - the Realm of Polarity: Pleasure & Pain, Right & Wrong.

The goal is to align these energies from the Central Sun and the Center of the Earth (above and below) in your heart.
* See grounding diagram to connect properly with the Earth.

The Central Sun is in the center of our galaxy and is the place from which our entire galaxy is orchestrated. It allows us to source cosmic energy directly into our bodies in the same way a plant photosynthesizes the sun for its nourishment. To handle this energy directly from the Central Sun, make sure your channel to the Earth is fully grounded (see the Grounding exercise).

* * *

When you get caught up in the horizontal landscape of drama (fear, pain, and suffering), you begin to swing like a pendulum between attraction and aversion. You swing in this horizontal plane like the tick-tock of a clock. Time becomes important. Attachments to things and people lead to greed, which gives rise to a type of insanity. These false cravings can never be quenched when you are in the "swing" of things. As this horizontal pendulum swings harder and faster, it swings further from its central point.

Staying vertically aligned has major advantages. You will find answers, and a sweet simplicity. You can remain poised in the present silence and open to the range of vibrations that exist simultaneously. You will still sway from side to side as you are continue to live in the horizontal plane, but it will no longer be a huge back-and-forth movement. It will become more like a circular momentum very close to the balance point, spiraling in on itself.

While experiencing your physical environment, you will still have preferences, but you can retain the central point of balance. That is the goal of the Vertical Alignment exercise. From the center, all knowledge is obtained, all cravings are quenched, and all love is unconditional and pervasive.

As you continue this practice on a regular basis, incredible gateways will open up. The longer you can sit in the center of your being, the more connected to the wave of synchronicity you will become. Even as the pendulum of life swings back and forth (in the horizontal plane), you can always find center via this simple practice of alignment.

This practice is non-negotiable. It takes precedence over everything else. It can happen with a simple thought, an intention, and a few breaths. The more you practice this Vertical Alignment, the stronger the frequency of your heart becomes.

Practicing in groups has enormous effects. It clears us of our lower natures and magnetizes us to our higher ones. It brings us back into wholeness and a true and complete healing of our bodies, minds, and souls.

As different aspects of your personality and conditioning fall off and away, things can become confusing. It can feel painful, like a part of you is dying. These moments, more than any others, are when you will need to fasten yourself to your ideal, to your heart, and to your truest desires—and hold steady.

I recommend you do this Vertical Alignment practice for 21 days in a row, without fail and without a break in the days, to experience miracles unfolding in your life.

For guided support with this exercise, watch my video online KnowTheSelf.com/video. Practice Vertical Alignment daily for extraordinary results.

Reclaim Your Imaginal Realm

In order to establish Vertical Alignment, you will need to activate your imagination. At some point when you were little, someone probably said to you, "Ah, that's just your wild imagination." From that moment on, you (like many people when they hear this) probably began to think of your imagination as a type of hallucination, a false reality.

Unfortunately, comments like that are why magic and synchronicity left your life, and why you stopped trusting your inner vision.

What you will find in using the keys I offer in this book is that the Imaginal Realm is your most important asset. Your imagination is a treasured resource, a muscle to exercise, and a tool for personal growth. However you want to refer to it, the imagination is the screen on which all unseen realities are projected.

As you learn to open your imagination and sync up with the river of life, you will understand the vital importance your imagination plays. Honoring your imagination and allowing it to build up muscle, to be free and wild, is essential for living in the flow.

See if you can catch yourself when you begin to diminish, shame, or blame your imagination. Notice if you say things like, "It was just my imagination," when you are trying to describe complicated feelings or things you see while in Vertical Alignment. Take a moment to reflect: Have you been diminishing, shaming, doubting, or blaming your imagination? Forgive yourself.

From now on, start honoring your imagination and let the beauty of your life pour in. As you begin to learn the language of your imagination, it will become a trusted ally and resource you can rely on for information.

The word "imagination," divided in two, becomes "image" and "nation," and that is exactly what happens inside the mind's eye. Imagination is the screen on which our souls communicate with us.

The first step toward building a strong imagination muscle is to reclaim the word, its use, and your connotations of it. Notice the items around you; for example, the furniture in your house, your computer, and your favorite pair of shoes. How did they come into being? The first step in innovation is imagination. Like the light bulb above a character's head in a cartoon that signifies a brilliant idea that pops in from nowhere, imagination literally pops into the mind's eye. Let's reclaim that word and remember Albert Einstein's wise words:

> Imagination is more important than
> knowledge. For knowledge is limited
> to all we now know and understand,
> while imagination embraces the
> entire world, and all there ever will
> be to know and understand.

Somehow, in our modern-day language, we have come to equate imagination with "making things up," but there is a difference. "Making something up," or "conjuring," is different from what I mean when I use the term "imagination."

"Imagination" is the spark of intuitive knowing; it is the screen on which Spirit communicates and on which the other dimensions are revealed. "Conjuring things up" is about pushing your will onto the screen of your mind's eye. For example, if someone says, "Imagine a tree," the tree in your mind's eye is a projected visual from conjuring. However, the type of tree you see and whatever animals or other elements might appear in the tree's environment are your pure imagination.

As you honor your imagination more, you will value it more and increase your intuitive capacity. Your capacity for understanding the difference between pure imagination and forced visuals will increase the more you practice.

Embark on a Path of Self-Mastery

You are a multi-dimensional being waking up to your own magical nature. Your human potential is immense. What would the world feel like if everyone honored synchronicity and flowed in the river of life to their divine destiny? I imagine people spontaneously waking up their unique genius and becoming much more positive contributors to society. I imagine we would be more honest, more loving, and more supportive—finding new ways to cooperate with each other. We might just live in a more peaceful world. Don't you agree? That is my desire, and why I am sharing these keys with you.

When I first opened to the river of life and allowed my inner senses to guide me, it took me on a quest following synchronicity breadcrumbs across the globe. I ended up on a wild ride studying with mystics, shamans, physicists, oracles, and yogis. I hung out in ashrams, visited countless temples and places of worship, practiced yoga, meditated all day for months and years on end, lived in seclusion, and even became a renunciate for five years. Finally, I began sharing my healing gifts with others.

Professionally, synchronicity has opened golden doors to new opportunities at every turn. These magical gateways allowed me to traverse many career changes swiftly without missing a beat. My personal pilgrimage to Israel introduced me to my first business partner and together, we opened one of the first Web design firms in San Francisco, specializing in virtual reality. My career as a digital photographer started with a chance meeting in the bank with my all-time-favorite fashion designer, Richard Sharpe. Shortly after meeting him, I became his personal photographer in Japan. After touring with him for years, photographing his fashion shows in Japan, I was invited to become the U.S. president of a Japanese art, culture, and spiritual magazine. Not long after that, I found myself in a role as a consultant on artificial intelligence for an enterprise software application, which later took me back to Japan and closer to my spiritual teachers.

After my father's passing, another serious course correction led me to go back to school to earn my first college degree—in consciousness, healing, and ecology with a focus on sustainable communities. That opened the door for me to re-emerge as a healer and a holistic land manager.

Moving to India with my then husband, Vivek, led me on another eight-year stint abroad, and my synchronistic train warp-sped into a whole other plane of existence. I had the privilege of managing a farm, running permaculture programs with local villages, developing intentional eco communities, hanging out in wildlife reserves, establishing retreat centers, and working alongside spiritual masters and psychic children. I offered workshops and spoke at spiritual conferences on the topics of expanding consciousness and spiritual farming. All of these relationships and golden opportunities came with a series of extraordinary circumstances.

People are often puzzled about how I maneuvered so many career changes so quickly. When they learn a bit about my story, they ask me two questions: "How old are you?" and, "What did you study in school?" My capacity to manage all these roles was simply informed by following the river of life. None of my life has been planned—not by me, anyway. Whenever I *did* make a plan, it felt like the Universe laughed in my face and catapulted me in the opposite direction.

What I discovered after activating my own star seed was that many wonderful new capacities appeared for me to tap into. Each time I let go of my personal agendas and flowed with the river of life, a new ability flowered. Each innate gift I found needed to undergo testing. Each skill needed to be tuned and mastered before I could offer it with confidence, in true service to the world.

Within your star seed, a multitude of abilities are stored. They will awaken when you tend your inner garden. These innate gifts are within all of us. Some of your gifts will be more developed than others.

* * *

While going through my own awakening process, I identified four stages of Self-mastery that allowed me to track my developmental level. These same stages are how I now help my students track their own progress.

Identify Your Level of Self-Mastery

These stages are designated and identifiable by you, your mentors, and your community. They are not linear stages because they spiral upward along the path of your soul's remembrance. In my Mystery School, I assist people in their transitioning between these levels of Self-mastery, but you can also track them yourself.

These are practices of Self-knowing that will tune you to your innate gifts so you can discover and harness your true potential and live out your divine destiny. I explain the stages below so you can understand and identify where you might be currently with your already-awakened abilities. The Four Stages are Student – Apprentice – Adept – Mentor.

The Student Phase. As a student, you are aware that you want to evolve and grow. You are aware of old wounds in need of healing. However, you may be carrying resentments and blame and feel challenged with difficult emotions. You are seeking greater purpose in life and want to know the truth beyond what the conscious mind is presenting. You are a curious truth-seeker in pursuit of potentials. You recognize your potential for living as essence, beyond the physical density of matter, and find books and guides to take you to the next level. The symbol I use for the student is an empty golden chalice, a magical vessel for which the nectar of your life's magic is being poured.

The Apprentice Phase. The symbol for the apprentice is the wand. The wand represents your pure kundalini power activated in your body and your innate gifts becoming manifest. At the apprentice level, you have experienced yourself as a spiritual being. You have done a lot of personal development work on your conscious wounding (the traumas and programming from childhood that you carry), and you have awakened to one or more of your extra senses. In this phase, you will have developed a mid- to high level of emotional intelligence and are fine-tuning your awareness for multi-sensory living. The apprentice phase is much like that scene in *Harry Potter and the Sorcerer's Stone* when Harry first receives his wand; he knows he has magic, but does not know how to wield it.

In this phase you have access to and can use your extra senses, but you use them through trial and error. You may not be in control of turning them on or off, and you lack confidence in your abilities. This is the stage when it's best to seek guidance, as you may be at risk of misusing your newly-found senses for personal gain or negative power dynamics.

In the apprentice phase, it is imperative to understand ethics and remember the purpose of your life. Your kundalini energy needs to be fine tuned and directed in order for you to use your gifts responsibly.

The Adept Phase. The symbol for the adept is the sword. It represents a cleared mind, one that can pierce through illusions to see and speak the truth. As an adept, you have anchored and merged with your immortal being as a palpable experience in your physical body and awakened your star seed. You are able to hold a high vibration of light in your body the majority of the time. You see that you are the cause of your reality and take full responsibility for all you create. You have impeccable integrity with your Self and in all your relationships. You have healed emotional, mental, and physical ills and have mastered the art of vibrational presence. You offer your spiritual gifts to others purposefully, and do so with accurate results time and again.

The Mentor Phase. The symbol for the mentor is the rose, the thorns representing the initiations that have been endured and transmuted into beauty. The scent of the rose expands the senses to all those who smell its fragrance; the thorns protect the vulnerable exposed spirit (flower) of the teacher. You have mastered your gifts and are able to teach and guide others to open their own with ease, clarity, and comfort. At this stage, you become a positive role model, an elder, a wise one, and a counselor for your community.

* * *

Throughout life, we spiral around these phases of Self-mastery with each discovery of new gifts that emerge. Some of our gifts may be unlocked, developed, and mastered fully, while others go through various rounds of learning. Multiple stages can be present simultaneously.

As long as we are on this planet, we are forever students, and this process is continuous. There is never a point of full arrival. When you think you have arrived at mastery, that is the moment you begin as a student once again.

Awaken Other Ways of Knowing

As you awaken to your innate genius and follow synchronicity, paranormal phenomena and full sensory experiences will occur. There is a whole world of paranormal gifts and innate abilities to explore. I've included a glossary of terms below so you can familiarize yourself with and understand the differences and similarities of the words and concepts and define your own abilities better.

While reading the list, notice which senses of yours might be more active than others. We all have the ability to activate innate senses. In the coming years, as more people activate their star seeds, we will find spontaneous sensory awakenings happening all over the world.

You can stop being afraid of your innate knowing and learn to cherish this ability in yourself. These gifts are your doorway to waking up, to the next phase of our collective human evolution.

Alternate Ways of Knowing:

- **Clairvoyance**: This is the ability to see things in your mind's eye. What you see often plays like a movie, whether your eyes are open or closed. It is the psychic ability to see, and people with this ability are often referred to in ancient texts as "seers."
- **Clairaudience:** This is the ability to hear direct messages. The information comes in as an aural sound to the one sensing. It can sound like a voice inside the head or it may actually be felt outside of the head, in the environment as sound vibrations.
- **Clairsentience:** This is the ability to receive messages via feelings and emotions. Clairsentient people are great empaths, understanding psychically through body sensation and emotions.
- **Claircognizance**: The ability to know things psychically without logic or facts.
- **Clairalience:** The ability to smell while in a psychic reading, or meditative state, such as smelling the perfume of a departed soul.
- **Clairgustance**: The ability to taste while in a psychic reading, or meditative state, such as tasting the favorite food of a departed soul.

Other Abilities Described as Paranormal Phenomena:

- **Trance Mediums/Channelers:** The ability to communicate at will with disincarnate beings or other sentient life forms.

- **Lucid Dreaming:** Waking up while in a dream state enough to know that you are dreaming, and being able to consciously change the dream.
- **Astral Travel:** The ability to project yourself out of your body to another time and place on the astral plane (be it on the other side of the planet, another dimension, or next door).
- **Past Life Memory:** The ability to remember other lifetimes and timelines that occurred in your soul's memory bank. The existence of this phenomenon is highly debated, with many explanations for how it happens, but thousands of cases have been verified via research and historical facts.
- **Telepathy:** The ability to perceive another person's or animal's thoughts and to communicate directly between minds.
- **Teleportation:** The ability to project yourself (with your body intact) to another place in the Universe (Just like "Beam me up, Scotty" on *Star Trek*).
- **Bilocation:** The ability to duplicate your physical body and be present and visible in two locations simultaneously.
- **Precognition**: The ability to see into future events.
- **Psychokinesis/Telekinesis**: The ability to influence external objects or events without the use of physical energy.

Yogic States of Awakening:

- **Kundalini Awakening:** This is a physical experience of waking up stored life force energy that lives at the base of your spine, coiled like a sleeping serpent. When activated, this energy rises up your spine. It can feel like a big rush of energy, a lightning bolt, or a high-vibrational tingling that wakes up extra senses as it passes through the various channels in the body.

- **Siddhis:** Supernatural perceptual states of awareness reached by trained yogis. Directly translated from Sanskrit as "perfection," "accomplishment," "attainment," "success." There is a very long list of Siddhis (powers) described in the ancient Vedic texts; below I've listed just a few. Siddhis are awarded to yogis who have reached great attainment on their spiritual path based on their "samskaras" (soul development) from previous births. A partial list of Siddhis includes: knowing the past, tolerance of heat and cold, reading minds, remaining unconquered by others, being undisturbed by hunger, control over bodily functions and thirst, the ability to hear or see things far away, teleportation and astral travel, shape-shifting (taking any shape one desires), conscious dying (at one's own will), making oneself the size of an atom, becoming weightless, becoming infinitely heavy, having unrestricted access to all places, communing with ascended masters and gods, and perfect accomplishment of one's desires.

- **Samadhi:** This is the ultimate goal of meditation. It is union with the monadic soul ("I AM" presence). It happens when the mind becomes single-pointed and the yogi returns to oneness and bliss. This is the full flowering of consciousness.

Can you imagine what life would be like if we were to teach our children—from a young age—to access all their senses and live out their divine destiny? What would it be like to live in a world where people were healed of their traumas and had awakened their star seed? I hope that by reading this book and practicing the keys contained within it, you will join me in this vision to heal our mental programs and awaken to our divine destiny.

If you have questions about your extra senses or want to share your experiences with me, feel free to email me at info@knowtheself.com. If you would like to study your own Self Mastery in the Mystery School, check my website for upcoming sessions www.KnowTheSelf.com

Create a Soul Journal

As you meditate and complete the exercises in this book, your imagination will be reactivated. You will begin to see stories, situations, colors, words, and symbols as your imagination dialogues with you. It will be helpful to note it all down in your journal to document your process and your progress.

Synchronicity often occurs as cryptic messages from your soul, but sometimes they are crystal-clear directives. Make sure to write it all down, no matter how small or insignificant it might seem at the time. You never know how important it might turn out to be for understanding something vital.

Your synchronistic patterns will become stronger as you put them together; they will weave an interesting and fantastic trail to your life's true purpose. Your Soul Journal will become a resourceful guide to your divine destiny as you chart your trials and tribulations, along with your visions, dreams, and ideals.

Your intuition uses the muscle of your imagination to communicate to you, so pay close attention to all the little messages you receive and notice how you respond or react to them. Are you trying to silence your intuition, or do you ignore it altogether? Are you minimizing what you imagine? When you ignore your gut instincts or your intuition, what happens? See if you can stay in equanimity and just take notes in your journal.

Along the process of awakening your star seed, your journal will end up cataloging the stories, direct downloads, and synchronicities of your life. Make time to write in your journal, and treat your completed journals with the same respect you would a holy scripture. Your journals may very well contain the keys for your future self to prosper.

Every now and then, go back through your Soul Journal; read it, highlight insights, and look for recurring themes or patterns appearing. In time, you will see how you are being guided. There are a number of ways to journal that can deepen your practice. Here are a few of my favorites:

- **Question and Answer:** Pose a question to your soul and listen deeply for the response. Begin writing each word as it arises in your mind. Do not edit or change what is instinctually revealing itself; simply write the response that arises as it comes through. You might also try writing questions with your right hand on the right side of the paper and answering with your left hand on the left side of the paper.

- **Automatic Writing:** Simply put your pen to the paper and allow yourself to start writing. You could begin with, "I am trying an exercise in automatic writing . . ." and then allow your pen to keep flowing, keeping your hand moving. You may start scribbling or end up with garbled letters, or you just might find words appearing as if by magic. Explore this process for at least ten minutes and see what wants to come through.

- **Dream Tracking:** Keep a journal or voice recorder next to your bed. When you wake up in the morning, before getting out of bed, write every detail of your dream, or speak it into the recording device. Later, once you are awake and out of bed, use your analytical mind to decode it.

- **Personal Inquiry – Diving into Deeper Truths:** This is similar to the Q & A I mentioned earlier, but going deeper within to challenge your beliefs. When you answer one question, pose another one, and continue diving deeper and deeper into the truth of the matter, as if you are your own therapist. You can use Byron Katie's four questions to get you started. Find a situation in your life that is bothering you, then ask her four questions to challenge the belief you have around the situation:

  Is it true?

  Can you absolutely know that it's true?

  How do you react, what happens, when you believe that thought?

  Who would you be without the thought?

- **Emotional Expression:** Allow your crazy and wild self to go at it on the page, exposing your deepest emotions, the ones you fear may come out of your mouth toward another. This is a great way to discharge energy around challenging relationships and situations in which you feel victimized or unable to express yourself fully. After you've written down all your feelings, take a break. Later, look back at what you wrote with a fresh mind, from a clearer state, and make sense of it all. See how you feel.

- **Tracking Emotional and Mental Processes:**
  This type of journaling will help you track your emotional weather and become aware of habitual emotional and mental patterns. Use a calendar to note your feelings every day. You will begin to see the cycles you go through, the ups and downs, and after a few months, you will be able to see larger emotional and mental patterns at play. Notice the moon cycles along with your thoughts and feelings, and see if you notice patterns and mental habits. Or, if you are into astrology, you can add a more complex layer of tracking the planets in transit along with your emotional state. For menstruating ladies, this is a great tool to aid in the wisdom of your own moon cycle and enhance your energy flows.

* * *

There are times when it is really complicated to follow synchronicity, and the symbols can trip you up. I'll give you a recent example from my own life of how I got stuck on a superstitious tangent and had to override fear.

Foxes have long been associated with tricks and illusions in my mind, and I have always viewed them as a dark omen. For years now, if a client has asked me about fox medicine, I have always told them to be very cautious and discerning. So, you can imagine the confusion that ensued for me, over several months, when the following synchronicities occurred.

It started a few days after flirting with a guy I was dating when I told him he was foxy. It's not a term I have ever used with a man, but it felt appropriate to his personality. Then I saw seven foxes in a 24-hour period—seven! There were three crossing the road together about ten miles away from my house. Then there were two more just another 100 feet up the road. As I can go months without spotting any, this was already rather remarkable. When I walked into my home, I quickly jumped online to read up on fox medicine.

My friend Claudia messaged me on Facebook, distracting me mid-search. We text chatted for a few minutes and then, as she signed off, she sent me a sticker emoji—of a fox! I hadn't mentioned anything to her about the guy I was dating, or what I had been researching when she reached out, or any of my fox sightings! I wondered if she was unconsciously sending me a warning.

Somehow, I felt her sticker was an omen and that I seriously needed to pay attention. I was feeling really uneasy, feeling the trickster in its full glory getting the best of me. I started racking my logical brain about why she would send me a fox emoji, for it wasn't sitting well with me, until I remembered that she had used "fox" as her pen name years prior. However, the whole thing seemed so perfectly timed that deep down I knew it was way too synchronistic to dismiss all these signs.

The next morning, some friends came to visit, and a few of us were walking around the property together. As we passed through the gate, we had to carefully step over some scat on the ground. One of the guys said, "Looks like a bobcat was here," and I instantly chimed in without thinking, "Nope, it's a fox."

Now, what the hell did I know? I had no idea what fox droppings look like, and at that point, I had never actually seen a fox on the property. Was I just obsessed with the previous day's fox sightings, which occurred miles away? Well, just as I was wondering about my own know-it-all comment, my friend's son ran right past me, and I immediately noticed his hat. He was wearing a red-tailed fox hat! I took a photo and added it here for you to see. This is how it always happens, multiple signs pointing me along a wild roaming path. For me, the boy in the hat fully confirmed my strong intuitive sense that the scat was indeed from a fox, although I had no scientific proof. I knew that the trickster was playing games with me, and I couldn't stop giggling and feeling baffled.

The games continued. The following week, every day as I went out to water my garden, there was a half-eaten apple near my watering can. Each time I found it, I would throw it back under the apple tree, out of my way. Then the next day, another apple would be back near my watering can. I felt like I was playing hide and seek with some little creature, but I had never seen him. Was it really a fox? Do foxes eat apples? What was going on here? Deep inside, I truly felt it was a fox, again with no hard proof, just a "knowing."

Another week or two passed and I started finding more and more scat each day along my walking path, as well as at the gate where I had to stop to unlatch it each time I entered or left the property. And somehow, each time I saw the scat, I also knew, or quickly learned, something about my new boyfriend. In one instance, I sensed intuitively that he was coming to surprise me for a visit; in another few instances, I came to "know" that he was sharing something private about our relationship or being cute or foxy with another woman, as is his nature. In those moments, I would call to check in with him and I found I was always correct about my intuitive "knowing" assumptions.

These trickster antics continued. One day, I walked out of my cabin to the base of an ancient hollowed-out Redwood tree that I use as my meditation sanctuary. Inside of the hollow I kept two objects, my Tibetan singing bowl and a wooden mallet that I used to strike it. I first noticed that my wooden mallet had been moved about 20 feet outside the tree. Then I discovered that the little fox had defecated directly inside my Tibetan singing bowl! I was aghast, yet I couldn't stop laughing and feeling special at the same time. It was quite comical.

The trickster antics continued over the next month. Each instance with the fox was timed perfectly with my boyfriend and our push/pull dynamic. One day I got so angry with him that I told him I wanted to break up. The next morning, I awoke to find fox scat on my front doormat! (See photo; that's a banana slug on it.) It made me laugh, and in my heart, I forgave the fox instantly. These antics had become absurd and ridiculously cute, yet I was still curious as to why the animal was playing games. It aroused my suspicions and kept me on guard with my new boyfriend. Those synchronistic shenanigans were keeping me hyper alert to whom I was dealing with.

At night, I began leaving a dog biscuit on my front doorstep to see if I could actually sneak a peek at the mysterious animal trailing me. Each morning, the biscuit was gone. I would sit in front of my window for hours, waiting for him, and even wake up in the middle of the night to take a peek outside, hoping I'd spy a creature eating it, but no luck. Another few days went by, and I wondered if I was going a bit crazy living so far out in the woods on my own. Maybe the scat wasn't from a fox after all? Maybe a squirrel or a raccoon was taking the biscuit?

Things came to a head with my new boyfriend. On a particularly difficult day, he was traveling out of state, and this time, I got angry—*really angry*. I had had enough of his foxy nature. I was screaming at him and felt totally self-righteous in my accusations. He was tricking me, right? There I was, a puddle of mush on the floor, sobbing, wanting to know the truth, so I prayed for a miracle—out loud. I actually screamed loudly cause my nearest neighbor was over 30 acres away, and I wanted to feel into my depths. Within an instant, something made me stop screaming and look out the window. What did I see? A fox sitting on my doorstep! In that moment, I melted. My anger fell away, and I felt my boyfriend's sincerity and understood more about his foxy nature. He wasn't a bad guy per se; he was a lawyer and a cute fox. He just liked to play around and keep me guessing.

The next morning, I felt a huge cloud had lifted. I began trusting the reasons I had chosen to date the guy in the first place. I stopped fighting with my own inner demons and took responsibility for all the ways I had been blaming him. Fox medicine teaches us how to get around difficult obstacles, how to find the sharpest and smartest solution to any problem, and how to master resistance.

The next day, as I was writing about twin flames and soul mates, the fox appeared on my doorstep once again. He stayed put for a while and acted like he wanted me to pet him. I opened the door and got a good look at him, from no more than an arm's length away. He even let me take his picture. (See photo on next page, you can watch a video of the fox when you download the workbook). When I sent the photo to my foxy boyfriend later that evening, he was really surprised. At that very moment, he was talking about synchronicity and foxes with a woman he'd just met who happened to be wearing a fox-fur coat! When he got my text, he showed her the photo; apparently, she got a bit freaked out by all of this.

He and I started talking about this amazing moment of synchronicity, and I was curious about who this woman in the fancy fur coat was and why he was walking around town with her. Just at that moment, as I was asking him about the mystery lady, the fox came back to my doorstep and wanted to be fed again! Luckily for my boyfriend, I was distracted. He got away without answering a direct question, as he was a master of evasion. Even so, I began to relax, understanding the beauty of his foxy nature and his professional training.

It took me three months to understand what that little fox was trying to teach me. He cleverly turned things around, made me laugh, and taught me that I can adapt, be flexible, and move through obstacles and resistance quickly—if I choose to. During arguments with my boyfriend, I realized I had become rigid, fearful, fixed in my thinking, and demanding in my needs. It was closing me off to love and had me reacting from fear. Superstitions breed fear, so it became obvious that I needed to face my fears.

The fox is a charmer who heals others through laughter, play, and illusion. The fox loves to entertain and keep people guessing. He has shown me that I can skate between worlds, on the edges, and enjoy it. He has brought me potent medicine, along with a furry new friend.

When I feared the fox was a bad omen, I

reminded myself that love reigns supreme and that I cannot be hurt, except by my own design. It isn't easy to let go of the negative things I have heard about foxes, but I now trust my inner guidance, which is full of wonder and love.

Just after writing this story, I received an email from The Shift Network with a new course offering from Caroline Casey entitled, *The Way of the Trickster*. In the email it was written, "discern the difference between the Con-Man and the Trickster (the latter liberates us from the former)... understand why the Trickster is key to your spiritual liberation and the liberation of our world, especially in times that are heavy and hard."

Needless to say, I signed up to learn more. Life offered me a mirror.

I'm sharing this story with you because it was a very strong synchronicity that occurred while I was writing this book. When we are connected to the river of life, the golden thread stitches up the space between us. We are alone when we are in our pain and suffering, but through joy and love, we find connection. We all come from love, we are love, and love is all around us. We only need to tap into that magical nectar and allow our sadness and fears to melt away.

When I choose love over fear, and watch with eyes wide open, the fox can never lead me astray.

Key #4
Find Your Balance

*"If you want peace, you don't talk to your friends. You
talk to your enemies."*
— Desmond Tutu

As you dive into the practices I've outlined in this book,
you will find that a few things begin to happen. You will
become very aware of your mental nature, especially
the incessant thoughts and curious emotions that
bombard you. As you practice radical honesty with
yourself and take responsibility for what you are
creating, you may find yourself at times depressed,
confused, or stuck in challenging emotions.

You can't always control your thoughts. In fact,
many of your thoughts are not your own but were
picked up in the airwaves, as conditions and
impressions that flowed in and out of your mind. In
order to align with the river of life so it can carry you to
your divine destiny, you will need to understand what
you are feeling and take responsibility for it. This may
sound easy, but it's not always that easy.

So much of the time, we become so conditioned
by thinking our way through life that we forget how to
feel. We often numb our feelings because they are too
intense or don't make sense to our logical mind.

Emotions can erupt from places inside that we didn't even know existed, without any apparent reason.

Taking time to sit in silence to allow yourself to feel is a critical component of aligning yourself to synchronicity. Whenever you sit still, emotions naturally arise, along with a stream of thoughts. When you sit still long enough, you eventually move beyond the thoughts and, ultimately, beyond the emotions; there, you will find yourself resting in your inner nature. When you arrive at that resting place, it is rejuvenating, peaceful, and perfect. But what about the rest of the time?

Understand Your Mental Make-Up

As psychoanalyst Dr. Eric Berne describes in the book *Games People Play: The Basic Handbook of Transactional Analysis*, the mind comprises three main ego states: child, adult, and parent. By identifying these three states of mind, you will be able to notice what is governing your egoic responses. This will help you understand yourself better when navigating the different emotions and thoughts that bubble up.

You have an inner child within you that dictates your feelings with sensations of needs and wants. This is where your demands, your exaggeration, and drama originate. You also have an adult mind within you that is more even-tempered and likes to make choices clearly based on reason. This adult within you is attentive, factual, and contemplative. It "chooses" things, rather than demanding them.

The third division of the mind is the parental mindset, which is split into two sides. One is the caring parent, which is unconditionally loving, kind, and patient with you. The other is critical and judgmental, impatient, and patronizing.

Once you understand that your mind is composed of these different levels of wisdom, you can begin to communicate among them and use these different aspects of your brain to help yourself along. For example, if you find yourself being highly emotional, e.g., filled with grief, sadness, or despair, you can identify how old that emotion feels within you. Often, emotions are trapped in a childhood memory.

Your mind plays tricks with your psyche, and your emotions live in multiple timelines within your history. It can really be confusing as parts of our psyche come up spontaneously to be realized and released. I'll share with you a few examples of how this happens.

One of my students was feeling a lot of grief and despair after a breakup with her boyfriend. Though it had been months since the breakup, she couldn't understand why she was overcome with such intense emotions. After helping her to get in touch with the depth of her feelings, I asked her how old she felt while experiencing the deep despair. Without much thought, she realized she was feeling the emotions of her six-year-old self. After further questions, she told me her father had passed away when she was six. She had felt abandoned, distraught, and ridden with grief, but her six-year-old self had been unable to handle the intensity of those emotions, so they remained buried deep in her unconscious mind.

After giving some space for those emotions to fully be released, I invited the caring parent within her to pick up the small child and soothe her pain. In doing this, she was able to cope with her pain and release the grief of her father's sudden passing. The pain of her recent breakup diminished, and she felt able to move forward without the despair she had been carrying. She was then able to use her adult mind to stabilize her feelings and open herself up to meeting a new man and so began dating again.

Here's another example. After beginning a daily meditation practice, another student of mine was having uncomfortable visions while deep in meditation. She didn't like the images she was seeing; they were strange sexual images of herself as a small child. She had no conscious memory of ever having been sexually abused, but each time she went into a deep meditative state, those images would appear. They were disturbing, and she no longer wanted to keep up her practice of meditation.

During our session together, she was able to recall one of those images consciously and slow down the pictures to become clearer about what actually was happening within her psyche. We discovered that the images were pieces of her childhood memory from which she had dissociated in order to protect herself. Once she was able to sit with the feelings that the images brought up in her, she was able to heal her inner child by caring for her and allowing her to emote. She brought this small child back home into her heart to align her with her true nature, and felt instant relief.

After our session, she was unable to find proof

that those repressed memories were actually true, but within her psyche, she felt cared for, soothed, restored, and somehow free of the tormenting images. The repressed memory made sense regarding a lot of relationship dynamics she was experiencing in her life and helped her come to terms with her previously unknown fear. Her meditation practice resumed, and the terrible images ceased to present themselves. She felt restored.

* * *

Identifying your mental make-up is very helpful in navigating the plethora of emotions and thoughts that bombard your psyche. Knowing which part of your brain is mostly in charge is crucial to finding, creating, and maintaining emotional balance. I have a simple worksheet you can download to help you understand this concept better; you may access it at: KnowTheSelf.com/workbook. Using this worksheet, you can draw your current mental state and begin to identify which part of your mind is most often running the show.

When you are able to switch between these mental states by choice, you will be more equipped to handle the pendulum swing of life. As you reclaim to your innocent nature, you return to the primordial garden where your wild nature is free, where your inner child is safe, where your adult is self-expressed, where your critical parent keeps you in line, and where your loving parent soothes old wounds.

As you learn how to balance, the extraordinary happens. Your health improves. You feel alive and vital, and you rejuvenate much more quickly. You embody latent powers and awaken the potential that lies within you.

Coming into balance is learning to live in a dynamic state, dancing with polarity. See if you can learn to ebb and flow, like the ocean.

Balance the Yin/Yang Within

When you confront the darkness in your life with a love that is equal to it, you can vibrate an enormous amount of light to illuminate your shadow. This light lets the shadow know how the two can dance in harmony with one another. Once the shadow recognizes the light, it is able to realize that it also has love inside itself, even if just a small spark.

As you meditate and move closer to the center of your soul essence and activate your star seed, there will be chaos, intensity, and heightened awareness. You may find yourself living inside a paradox of both light and dark. These two powerful forces are magnetized to each other and create a powerful dynamic akin to two magnetic poles holding each other in place.

There is no escaping the polarity in this dimension, no back door or roundabout way to fully experience balance. Balance is in the center, where the two aspects of your paradox meet. Feel into the line between the light and the dark to find your balance between the two.

When you are able to fully accept the most horrendous truths about yourself, about the dark aspects of your personality, that is the moment you flip to the other side and are able to invite your darkness into the light.

Relationships are the perfect mirror for inner growth. As you judge others, know that an aspect of you really needs your attention. When you are fully able to see the things you dislike in others as aspects of yourself, that is the moment of deep healing. This is not an intellectual pursuit; it is a physical, emotional, and spiritual resolve. This type of mirror work goes beyond forgiveness. This is the healing that comes after you forgive someone. This is when you fully accept the thing you despise and are able to forgive yourself. When you find aspects of yourself as the perpetrator, the enemy, the one who has caused you so much harm—when you are able to see aspects within yourself as as clearly as you see them in the person you dislike so much—that is the moment you experience transcendence. That is when you are able to go through the white dot on the dark side of the yin/yang symbol. That is when you come into harmonic resonance within yourself and return to your wholeness.

This balancing experience will happen again and again as you face your fears, judgments, and traumas and level up to various stages of your spiritual growth. When you arrive at this type of healing dynamic with your inner demons, your spiritual body evolves, and you awaken to higher states of consciousness.

Look to the ouroboros symbol of the snake biting its own tail to remember how you can merge with the part of yourself that you most despise. This level of self-forgiveness will heal you of your pain and suffering and offer you levels of balance that deliver you into transcendent states of equanimity.

Connect to the Unseen Hand

The question "Do you believe in God?" is a challenging one for many people of my generation. For people who have been wounded by their religion or grew up atheist, this question is also one they tend to avoid. While I am not here to promote any particular belief (other than that it is high time we activate our star seeds), it is imperative in dealing with higher states of consciousness that you find something larger than yourself to connect with and surrender to. I like to call on the image of God as Love or Divine Grace or simply The Unseen Hand.

Love is an energy I find easy to open to without getting my mind all tripped up in religious debate. While it's not always "easy" to surrender to love, it is an energy I respect and cherish and find immensely healing.

Try tapping into the love that exists in the space between us, those golden threads that hold life in perfect harmony. There is a lot of energy and information in the space between us, but focus on the strings of love. It might be easier for you to surrender to the word "Love" than to the word "God." Your term for this all-pervading energy might be different. You might find The Great Mystery, Universal Source, or Divine Mother more appealing. Whatever you choose to call this energy of life that animates us, it is helpful to have a word and a sense for what it means to you. Connecting to this overflowing, abundant energy source is imperative in overcoming obstacles when you sit face-to-face with horror and darkness. Faith in the unseen hand of love will help you navigate many challenges.

When you connect to Source, you will find the balance between darkness and light, you will encounter the zero point, a place between the negative and the positive where you are able to restore your faulty programs and receive a clearing of your electrical system. This moment of divine grace enables you to emerge in a state of newness with great clarity. Find the term that allows you to reference this all-loving presence, and create a relationship with it. By doing so, you will find a safe refuge and build up trust to follow the flow when life becomes difficult.

Declare Your Sovereignty

There is a lot of unconscious negative energy breeding all around us in the airwaves. This negativity can be attracted to you and picked up (by your own magnetic field) from your unconscious behaviors, through hereditary patterns, via governmental and societal conditioning, or even be placed there by malicious intent. When you don't heal your childhood wounds or ancestral wounds, or deal with the pain and distortions you carry, it attracts negativity and breeds with other similar programs like a virus. When we do not heal our own distortions, our field becomes twisted up. It also breaks into pieces and can contain small black holes that literally suck in energy toward itself, as these black holes are magnetic.

When we come in contact with other people with similar black holes, lower programs, and distortions in their field, our fields automatically exchange information, and all our programs communicate with each other. Negative programs spread like a virus. In the same way that germs spread between us, it is important to keep yourself clean and clear or unsuspecting energy patterns.

Because of this phenomenon, we are dealing with a society of negative programs that enslave us and trap our souls from knowing their true origin. It is my intention to help you liberate yourself from the insanity.

In order to take back your power and seal off your system to manipulative energy, you need to know how to declare your energetic sovereignty by creating a clear boundary around yourself. Whenever I let someone know I have a boundary and show them the line, I immediately feel them get defensive, and their own boundaries show up. This is a good sign; even though it can be uncomfortable at first, it is necessary. We all need boundaries to feel safe. Our personal boundaries are what differentiate our field from another's; they individualize us, and they are critically important.

A lot of New Age practices and liberal mindsets emphasize being "open." Open to new experiences, other people's ideas, new ways of thought, etc. Being open is a great concept, but it is a distorted concept when talking about one's personal energetic field. If your field is open and unchecked, you are vulnerable to manipulation by stronger energetic forces that want to control you. It is imperative that you learn how to protect yourself and define yourself (and your space) from others.

People who have experienced a lot of childhood wounding (the majority of people on the planet) have a lot of holes in their morphogenetic field. As such, the boundary around their body did not form properly during its development. Since this has happened to so many of us, it has left our fields open and vulnerable to outside influences who want to control us. It is imperative that we take back our power by healing and restructuring our energetic field.

As you open to new energy and new ways of seeing, it's important to create a safe container for your explorations. Whenever I discuss boundaries, I find many aspects of the self get activated. The extremist within will see things in black and white, good and bad, yes and no. Sometimes this shows up in our personality of being either "all in" or "over it and done with it." It often shows up as being self-righteous. This dismissive quality or obsessive compulsion is another way that boundaries (or lack of boundaries) show up in our life.

Then there's the blurry zone. This is the "I'm okay, you're okay" and "everyone and everything is okay" zone, which gives us a very permeable boundary.

We need boundaries to keep us safe, to define our perimeters. It helps us focus, grow, and harness our energy when we have a sense of safety inside our system. Take small children, for example. We tend to create safety for them. Whether it's through using a car seat, a playpen, or a security gate so they don't fall down the stairs, or simply giving them a bedroom in a house, we use boundaries to keep children safe from harm.

The boundaries I want you to re-establish are the ones you create and maintain in your morphogenetic field (refer to Key #3, the torus field illustration as a reminder of your morphogenetic field) . We each have a field around us that protects us and filters inputs on a constant basis, in the same way our bodies filter food into nutrients and waste. We don't see our digestion process happening; nonetheless, we know we have this ability.

Clearing your field consciously to ensure its health and wellness will speed up your soul's evolutionary process and bring you into flow safely and lovingly. More importantly, it will create a safe container for you and restore your sovereignty!

Many of my students come to me with their circuits blown out in their bodies, and their morphogenetic field is shredded from having pushed themselves too hard or from experiencing quantum leaps in their soul growth. My own awakening process was fast and furious, so I understand circuitry blowouts quite well. Learning how to restore my energetic boundary was something I learned the hard way, which is why I am on a mission to make sure people understand this very important reality. Our own field is what gives us our sovereignty or takes it away.

Let me explain further. As a multi-dimensional seer, I can view the energetic field around a body, and most people's field looks like a target with black holes piercing their container and welcoming in negative forces.

As we go through our day, we interact with a lot of energetic fields. A very small percentage of people's fields are healthy. For the most part (especially if you live in a city), the fields with which you interact all day long are distorted, chaotic, and in turn cause your field to run on overload. The field is magnetic, and it attracts energy that is like itself, so even the smallest tear or wound in your field is a window through which harmful energy may enter. Negative energy breeds like a virus from person to person. With all the electromagnetic pollution in the air, it further distorts our fields and makes us susceptible to a whole host of negative enslavement programs. Unless you live in a monastery, in an ashram, or off-grid deep in nature, these fields are exposing you to disturbances all day long.

It is a grim reality, but there is definitely something you can do about it. It is critical that you exercise dominion over your field. In order to find your own internal balance, illuminate your divine destiny, and remember your sovereignty, your field needs to be scrubbed clean, healed, and sealed. You want to be operating at the octave of harmonic resonance. When you are in tune and in sync with your own true nature, you can hold your own harmonic vibration and take back your power. How do you do that? It's actually your natural state, yet it takes dedication, practice, focus, and willpower to remember and keep it intact. It is important to stay attuned to your energetic field to keep it healthy, safe, and optimally functioning.

There are a number of ways to clear your field and erect a safe container. I am going to teach you what I find easiest. However, once you're able to set your own field and become innately familiar with it, you may very well find a faster, more efficient way. If you do, please share it with me!

You can take dominion over your morphogenetic field and create your boundary with your eyes open or closed, but while you are learning, it is easier to close your eyes. When your eyes are closed, you will feel more deeply, and your inner senses and other ways of seeing will wake up. In the following exercise, I will teach you how I discovered to become sovereign and heal my field of distortions. I suggest you practice this daily and as often as possible.

Become a Sovereign Being

1. With your mind's eye, draw a boundary around yourself the width of your outstretched arms. Make it a perfect circle, with your body positioned directly in the center with an equal distance all around.
2. Keep your attention, breath, and focus in your heart space.
3. Ask everything that is not you to step outside the circle. This includes other people's thoughts,

energy attachments, patterns you picked up, ideas of others, etc.

4. Ask your Inter-dimensional guides, angels, ascended masters, and any other beings of light that you work with to stand guard on the perimeter of your circle. You may not know you have guides, you may not be able to see them, but all light workers have spiritual allies working with us on the various planes of existence, so you can ask your allies to make themselves known to you and stand as a boundary to your energy field.

5. Allow this circle around you to pop into a perfect orb, encompassing your body. Keep the space inside your orb absolutely clear. You may want to sweep it out with an imaginary broom, or vacuum it up by plugging in a grounding cord. Get creative, and allow your imagination to show you how to keep this space clear. You will feel a subtle shift in your body when the clearing is complete; wait for this shift to happen. When it is complete, you will have an inner knowing. Some people can see it; others just feel it. Make sure you look above you, below you, and on both sides and clear every inch of your orb.

6. Once you have cleared your space, you are ready to ground your energy field. Complete the Vertical Alignment exercise and connect to the center of the Earth and the Central Sun, letting them merge and marry in your heart space. This is what births the magical star seed within you. Allow these two energies to pool in your heart,

mixing and merging, awakening your own small sun in the center of your circle.

7. Allow your small sun to shine like a pulsing star, pushing its rays out of your heart to fill up your circle all the way to the perimeter. Reclaim your space with your clear sovereignty—this is *your* space.

8. Allow the energy of your sovereign sun to clear your entire field of all negative programs, to awaken your crystalline nature and return you to perfect balance.

Do this exercise every day and as many times a day as possible. When this becomes your natural state of being, you will be completely free of any type of enslavement or external manipulation. You can listen to a 20-minute guided version of this on my website by going to www.knowtheself.com/video.

When you create your sovereign field, you will automatically be in the flow of synchronicity and activate your divine destiny. Failure to hold your orb clear in this way makes you susceptible to all forms of manipulation. The push-pull dynamic of the horizontal plane will not only keep you in suffering, pain, and drama, it will also keep you open to harmful energies being sent your way from your environment and people who have bad intentions or are simply unconscious. You can expand the clear, bright energy of your illuminated star seed to take up more space, growing your energetic field when needed, to blast out negative energy and harmonize a toxic environment. However, that is a more advanced technique, so start by simply allowing yourself to reclaim your own energetic field and sealing it off.

When you have successfully stabilized your own energetic field, wonderful things will begin to happen. The star seed within you that's carrying your potential will quickly take root, grow, and flower. It will awaken your inner genius and keep you safe from all harm. When this happens, your inner knowing will be activated and will guide you accurately.

Your star seed is already planted in the New Earth. When you can successfully hold this energetic form, you will wake up to the bigger version of yourself. You will become your own unique hub on the latticework of the golden thread that connects us. You will be the central sun in your own galaxy.

My friend, Yukiya, in Japan, refers to this awakening experience as becoming a "bliss ball," which is exactly what it feels like. You become a perfect orb full of light, feeling perfected bliss. Let's gather together and activate our clarity and shine as stars do in the heavens!

Clear Your Space

Now that you know how to establish sovereignty and create a safe boundary around yourself, I'd like you to apply the same technique to clear energy in a room, an entire house, or a building. Clearing space is really important to keep negative energies at bay. It provides a sweet, safe atmosphere that is highly charged with positive life force. It is great to clear a space before you conduct an intentional session, whether you are meeting with someone, hosting a party, needing to focus on something important, or just wanting the space to vibrate positivity.

A lot of people think they can't feel energy in a room, but we all can. It may take a little practice to notice *how* you feel it. Perhaps at work, for example, you have had that feeling when you walked into a conference room after a meeting ended and it felt stuffy and you could tell the meeting had been intense. Maybe you have walked into someone's house and could sense negativity there as if someone had been recently fighting or arguing. We each have this sense of knowing when something is not right. Sometimes you may notice a smell, or a strange humidity, a feeling that was left behind from the past. Pay attention the next time you enter a room, and use all of your senses to explore what you notice.

Our homes, bedrooms, and other environments need to be cleared because energy stagnates and will breed or attract negative patterns. Keeping a clean physical space is a great way to keep energy vibrating in a positive direction. Do you notice how fresh a space feels after a deep spring-cleaning? This is the type of environment in which we want to live, relax, and work.

Sometimes, we don't have time to clean the whole house, or we are in someone else's space and feel it is not our place to clean. In that case, there are plenty of other ways to clear a space that can work in everyone's favor— you don't literally have to pick up a broom. You can enjoy a deep sigh of relief if cleaning is not your thing, because this method does not take long, and it can even take place in your imagination—and it still works really well.

Take a few moments right now to try it out. In Key #3, you learned how to ground yourself and vertically align to the Earth and the Central Sun. You also learned how to create a safe energetic boundary. Now, you can do that for a room or an entire house, just as you would do for yourself. It is really simple; it just takes focus and clear intentions.

First, clear your personal energetic space (as described in Key #3), then apply the same technique to the entire room. Draw the perimeter around the room or entire house, drop the grounding cord to suck down all the stagnant energy, and allow the Central Sun to shine in a clear frequency of liquid light and restore the space to balance. The more you do this, the faster it will happen, and the more potent your space will feel. You will become a cosmic energy cleaner and do us all a great service. When people enter a cleared room, they will feel fresh, alert, and able to pay attention.

Sound waves also clear space and will change the frequency of a room. Playing music, toning with your voice, or using instruments are very helpful tools to change the feeling of a room quickly and set a good mood. There are many instruments that are wonderful space-cleansers for clearing lower programs that get trapped in a room.

Percussion instruments, like drums, will activate stuck energy, induce a trance state, and connect us to the rhythm of the Earth. Drums are very grounding and help unblock settled energy. The sound of a flute sweetens the energy of a space; it lifts our spirit and connects us with the birds and the elemental kingdom. The ringing of a bell will shatter dense energy and at the same time, it opens portals in the angelic realms and higher frequencies, depending on the sound of your bell.

Play around with various instruments and sounds to see what you sense and works best for you. You can simply use the sound of your voice to clear space by chanting, praying out loud, humming, or singing. If you are in a public place that is not accustomed to these space-clearing practices, such melodious antics might make you look like a strange hippie, so use discernment! This is not a magic show; it is a responsibility and the divine duty of awakened star seeds. If you feel a room needs clearing, it is your responsibility to clear it. Even the subtlest actions will have tremendous effects, so there is no need to make a display or call attention to yourself, just get the job done. This quote from J.D. Salinger sums up the job of an awakened star seed really well: *"She wasn't doing a thing that I could see, except standing there, leaning on the balcony railing, holding the universe together."*

Understand your environment and do what you can with what you have, and you will be doing us all a great service. You can listen to some of my favorite soundtracks that activate positive vibrations by going here: KnowTheSelf.com/workbook.

Another way to clear your space is by using water. Water is a master purifier. It instantly clears out static energy that gets stuck in the field. When you are processing a lot of energy in your field, make sure you are drinking enough water. It is also good practice to take showers often when you are going through challenging times or when your head feels clogged.

Whenever you feel lethargic, a shower will instantly cleanse the electrical currents in your body and will re-energize you quickly. If you happen to interact with a lot of people throughout the day by shaking hands, hugging, or simply talking, you may feel overly empathic or energetically porous. It is good practice to wash your hands all the way up to your elbows to clear whatever you have taken in through your hands. Even the act of sitting near water is helpful. Walking near a body of water, going to the ocean, swimming, or taking a bath will instantly refresh your energetic field and bring you back into a harmonic balance. You will especially feel this if you are having an emotional day. Submerge yourself in water, or at least place yourself near it, to soothe your senses and restore your calm.

Certain types of smoke and scents also clear the space. Burning candles, incense, sage, Palo Santo, frankincense, cedar, or sweet grass and using essential oils are other ways to clear negative energy from a room and restore beauty and harmony quickly. Find scents that smell good to you. If you feel nauseated or allergic, obviously that is not your medicine. Find the smudges and essential oils that work with your own constitution. Simply follow your nose to find what works best for you. Smudging the aura of a person helps to clear negative programs and thought forms. You can also smudge the entire room and especially the corners and doorways to keep the energy vibrant.

* * *

Using these simple space-clearing techniques, you will be able to maintain a high-vibrational field that will help you stay balanced and in the flow of life. By clearing space in a room, or an entire building, you are helping other people step into a clear field and feel energized rather than tired. Try this at home with yourself and your family as part of your weekly house cleaning routine.

As the masterful Swami Kriyananda states, "Your environment is stronger than your will." Often, we enter into negative places and no matter how hard we try, we cannot clear enough space for our energy field to stay healthy (the way I was feeling in Oakland before my house fire). In these toxic environments, the negativity has become so strong that our personal efforts to keep our own field clear are challenged. In such circumstances, it is best to remove yourself and go to a place where you can restructure your field, a place where things are already in harmony. This could be a sacred site or a place of worship. For me, it happens fastest when I enter deep nature, the more wild and dense the landscape, the better. When walking among old-growth forests, the harmony of the natural world instantly restores my field faster than any meditation practice or space-clearing technique I can muster. Mother Nature is already in perfect balance, so commune with her as often as you can. She will help you restore your original frequency.

Key #5
Magnetize Your Soul Group

"You find peace not by rearranging the circumstances of your life, but by realizing who you are at the deepest level."
– Eckhart Tolle

No one in particular told me what follows. This is my own personal understanding, based on my firsthand experiences. These ideas I share come from having powerful, life-altering visions that included an extensive series of past life regressions in which I experienced the things I describe. Over the past five years, my understanding has deepened through meditation and synchronistic conversations with friends and teachers, and later by a number of my own clients who went on to describe similar experiences in our regression sessions together. I encourage you to explore your own meditations and inner wisdom around this information. Our soul connections are beyond what we have been taught by books. The truth lies deep in our souls, and it is in our meditations that this knowing resides.

It's no secret that we live in amazing times. From global changes in political regimes to major innovations in technology, this is an exciting period to be a part of.

However, it's also just the beginning of a new experience here on planet Earth. As a small percentage of people all over the world are beginning to reawaken to their divine nature, we find ourselves at a crossroads.

We are searching for truth and our own inner light to guide us to the next stage of our development, but there is a plethora of teachers, choices, and beliefs out there. It can be really difficult to *know* with certainty what to believe and what we *should* be doing. The important thing to remember is that you are exactly where you need to be. There are a number of paths to take that will lead you to the truth. There are no *"shoulds"*; there is only potential.

At the same time, as you open up to new possibilities, it's vital that you learn to trust yourself and find the confidence and conviction of your own journey. There are still so many people living in fear instead of leading with their hearts. Roads that lead to destruction or wisdom can be found at every turn, and it's up to you to create a path toward conscious evolution. You must reimagine yourself as you truly want to be in order to begin the process of awakening your full potential.

Waking up is a choice to which you must commit yourself every day. When you come to understand that it is an internal process, and something that is within your own control, you can begin taking action. What is most important is that you find a way to establish your inner guidance system. As you create a personal connection with your soul's knowing, "help" will arrive in myriad forms. While your ego self is stuck in feelings like *anxiety, doubt, or looking for quick fixes to numb out,* the help that shows up is inter-dimensional and can transcend space and time. It comes from the *other side of the veil*, so to speak, where Infinite Love is the law, and abundance is the natural state of being.

Two things are important for you to know as you read this chapter. First, you are loved deeply on a universal level. When you are willing to open up and receive love, you will become closer to your divine nature and the group support that is discussed here. Second, you have help and guidance. You are not alone in your journey. This lifetime (the one you are reading this in) is all about connecting with your own inner truth as the entire planet starts the process of awakening. If you want help, you will find it. Trust that it is there, waiting for you to receive it.

As your star seed activates, you may soon realize that the *Golden Network,* which your soul is a part of, has been waiting for you to awaken. This soul group network is the unseen foundation of the grand cosmic orchestration that holds the chaos of your life in perfect order.

When a soul descends to Earth, it arrives here as part of a larger soul group called a *Monad.* The *Monad* makes up the mighty "I AM" presence, which you may have experienced in your meditations or perhaps read about in spiritual texts.

The *Monad* is easiest to describe as a collective group consciousness, meaning it is not a *physical* group of *people.* Some souls in your *Monad* may be in physical bodies; some (many perhaps) are on the other side of the physical veil. Your *Monad* is a group of souls that exist within multiple dimensions that are not bound by time, space, or single planets. This gets a little complicated, and instead of making it overly complex, the important relationship to understand between you and your own *Monad* is that the *Monad* acts as the Oversoul for your soul group. It is the resonance of all of you combined, like a hive-mind. Philosophers have spoken of an Oversoul for centuries. To fully ascend is to consciously return to your *Monadic* nature.

You can become aware of the presence of your *Monad* when you come into harmonic resonance with your own divine nature, which allows you to vibrate in harmony with the other members of your soul group. Such resonance has little to do with where its members are physically located (again, we are inter-dimensional beings); rather, it happens when each member connects through the vibrational frequencies of their awakened hearts (awakened star seeds). Activating your star seed is accomplished through focused intention and practice. It is a muscle you need to train. Since you can't just pick up a phone and dial your soul group, setting strong intentional desires and focusing on your own star seed activation is the main way to create a solid connection.

Within each *Monad,* there are 144 individual star seeds, known as your *Soul Mates,* who are divided into twelve groups of twelve. Within each group of twelve, there are six pairs of divine complements within your soul mate cluster. Within each divine complement, one soul holds a masculine polarity and the other a feminine polarity (the masculine/feminine soul essence has little to do with the gender you took at birth, each incarnation can be different). However, what I and other channelers have discovered is that your soul essence does not change. So, it is very possible that you could be a man with a feminine soul essence in this lifetime, or vice versa.

Your divine complement is your most harmonic soul mate. Whether this complement is in human form or not is irrelevant to their role in your life. They exist to assist you in your soul mission. It is possible that you are both the same gender in this lifetime; however, one of you will be holding the masculine essence and the other will be holding the feminine. When meeting this person, you will feel a very strong attraction and energetic compatibility. This is a deeply loving and rewarding relationship that can result in a long-term partnership on a number of levels. It can show up as a spouse, a business partner, or a family member. No matter what the circumstances are, there is always a sense of deep friendship that bonds these two complements together and a strong sense of loyalty that keeps them connected.

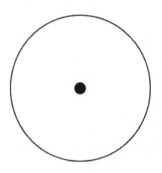

Become the Eye of the Storm

When you practice the Vertical Alignment meditation and star seed activation I covered in Key #3, you automatically begin magnetizing your soul group to a higher level of functioning. When you awaken, you help your entire *Monad* evolve and awaken. It is very powerful to use the symbol above as a Yantra Meditation. A Yantra Meditation is a Hindu practice to unlock cosmic keys of mystical diagrams, often geometric forms, like the popular Sri Yantra with which you may be familiar. These ancient symbols activate us on a soul level far beyond our mental comprehension. The only way to learn this tool is to practice it. Much of the information I am sharing with you in this book comes from doing my own yantra meditations with these symbols.

Focus on the Flower of Life

The symbol above is called the "Flower of Life." It depicts the soul group formation on an energetic, anatomical, and monadic level.

The Flower of Life is a widely used symbol found all over the world in our ancient cultures. The oldest discovery, which may be as old as 10.500 B.C., is in the Temple of Osiris in Abydos, Egypt, where it appears to be burned very precisely (and mysteriously) into the rock. The symbol is also found in the Forbidden City in Beijing, China, under the paw of the guardian lion, which is there to protect the dynasty. These lions are known as the guardians of knowledge. This symbol also appears in Turkey in the City of Ephesus. In Israel, you will find it in the ancient synagogues in the Galilee and Mesada. You will find this symbol in prehistoric art and carved in ancient temples in Greece. Italy, Spain, Ireland, India and Japan. This symbol holds the geometric language of our soul's origin and contains the blueprint of our soul's full potential.

The Flower of Life is a fifth-dimensional expression of the six complementary pairs of twelve souls, which make up one soul group. *We do not all belong to the same soul group or the same monadic group.* The *Monad* wakes up when we reach the perfected resonance within one soul group.

Let me explain. When twelve dedicated soul mates create harmonic resonance within themselves, they will activate the central thirteenth circle of the group, which is our collective hive mind. When we hold our fields in perfected resonance, we create a harmonic frequency that opens the fifth dimension and the ability to speak, hear, and receive information directly from our *Monadic* nature. When these twelve awakened star seeds resonate together and form the Flower of Life configuration in the fifth dimension, we instantly awaken the larger monadic group of 144. The harmonic resonance of the twelve will ripple out to the entire *Monadic* group instantly.

If you want to learn what this symbol represents for you, meditate by dissolving yourself into the center of it to find a deeper awakening (do a Yantra Meditation). Unfortunately, the innate part of you rarely communicates in words. As such, this may seem challenging to understand at first, but the more practice you commit to enhancing your soul communication, the deeper your understanding will become.

To practice, print out the Flower of Life symbol. You can find it on the Internet, or draw it out one circle at a time. Below you will find how to draw out the *Seed of Life* representing the six complimentary pairs and the foundation of the soul group. Place the symbol on a wall in front of you, right at eye level, and stare at it with relaxed eyes for as long as possible. You can ask questions of the symbol and allow it to share its wisdom with you. Track whatever you discover.

This image is made up of interlocking circles. Imagine yourself as one of those circles. Sit in the center of your circle (as the dot in the eye of the storm) with your boundary perfectly defined. Once you have established this, you can interlock your circle with those of your soul group, drawing the Seed of Life, which, as it extends, becomes the Flower of Life symbol. When this energy becomes grounded in your field and your energetic muscle is fully developed, you will eventually unlock the genius of your *Monad*. It is a powerful awakening when the *Monad* speaks to you, and even more amazing when it speaks *through* you.

The Flower of Life symbol spoke to me. It explained that it represented the Golden Network completely restitched, all awakened souls gathered in perfect harmony. When we all awaken together, we create this beautiful golden blossom of inter-dimensional consciousness, which transcends any knowledge you could obtain from a book or learn from a teacher. It gives you direct knowing of the Akashic records, the wisdom of all souls combined. Practice this Yantra Meditation, and please share your findings with me.

* * *

How do we better understand the concepts of soul groups, magnetization, Golden Networks, and vibration? Every human carries a specific vibration. The human body, biologically speaking, is electrical and gives off an electric impulse. This interacts with the Earth's electromagnetic field. The goal is to come into a harmonic resonance within yourself and with the earth (vibrating in sync with the Earth's magnetic field). When we are in harmonic resonance, it actually creates a frequency shift in the environment around us. Pretty cool, right? In essence, when we each take responsibility for our own field (imagine holding your energy like a dot in the center of your personal circle), our frequency reaches a state of harmony. When a group of us who have individually created harmonic resonance come together, we create a group resonance, which has an exponential effect on magnetizing our soul group. Through our combined efforts, there is the potential for spreading light and awareness and literally shifting everyone on Earth to a higher state of awareness.

In 2015, a group of us learned about the results of a mass transcendental meditation study, conducted in 1993, that was found to have reduced crime in Washington DC by 23 percent. We also read about similar results found for reducing violence in war-torn areas of Lebanon. As a result, were excited to see if we could create a similar effect, so we organized a free event in Oakland. Close to 1,500 people gathered that day to meditate together and bless Lake Merritt for World Water Day (you can read the full report of all that happened that day at BlessTheLake.com). Oakland is an area in which gang violence, racial injustice, and gentrification threaten peace. We synced up our live meditation and streamed our Oakland event online to hundreds of thousands of people internationally, all meditating simultaneously for peace. This collective meditation was incredibly powerful.

The electromagnetic frequencies all around us affect our consciousness. If we consciously recreate our own EMF around our body (as I explained in Key #4, *Become a Bliss Ball*), we can deflect the negative effects of everyday objects, people, places, and situations and be a blessing to those with whom we come into contact. Our televisions, Bluetooth devices, Wi-Fi broadcasts, and radio signals really harm the energetic field around our body, which makes it more challenging to come into harmonic resonance and sovereignty. However, by practicing the exercises in this book, you can strengthen your field and consciously create a positive EMF field around your body that resonates in harmony with nature and actually assists your soul group to raise the frequency of the planet and de-escalate the harmful effects of the EMFs.

In fact, getting into harmonic resonance opens you up to totally new possibilities, as it will unlock your human potential. The more you live in harmonic resonance, the more you will find yourself liberated from negative effects as you take control of your sovereign nature. When you become that dot in the center of your circle and own your energetic field taking dominion over your space, you will open your multi-dimensional nature and attract your Soul Group and *Monad* to you. This is the biggest service we came here to participate in—to restitch the Golden Network.

It is time that we utilize the power within us to consciously ripple out our perfected and healed fields to create the world we dream of. You might be wondering how many of us need to do this before we reach total resonance. I am not certain, but what I do know is that exponential growth happens when the right people with the right souls activate. For example, one person might be a very evolved soul and have the ability to offset and activate thousands, or even hundreds of thousands, of other souls. Another person with a different level of soul growth may only offset a handful. What I have seen is that when just twelve people reach harmonic resonance, miracles happen. So, let's not get worried about the exact numbers, but, rather, do our best to keep our own field clear and sovereign.

What I do believe is that we are dealing with the hundredth monkey effect, or what Rupert Sheldrake refers to in his book, *A New Science of Life; The*

Hypothesis of Formative Causation, as "morphic-resonance." When certain learned behaviors of a group of people (or animals) reaches a resonant number, the entire species suddenly knows that behavior. Remember, your spiritual practice positively impacts the entire planet.

Restitch the Golden Network

You will be attracted to other souls who hold a frequency that your system needs to experience in order to remember your true nature. All your drama in life is chaos looking for its balancing complement. Yes, there is an order to it. The patterns that you go on repeating and creating are all attempts to come back to wholeness and return to your soul group. I believe that if you are reading this book right now, you most likely have a divine mission that is being activated within your heart to reconnect with your soul group.

When you establish your energetic sovereignty, and can resonate in your own unique frequency, you will ride a wave to your divine destiny. Along the way, you will create the latticework of golden threads that connects your soul group back together. When you meet others in your soul group, your souls will push, pull, magnetize, and polarize as they seek a higher order. Much like the hub of a wheel, we must hold on to our own center by living out our personal visions, passions, and unique set of values. Like spokes radiating from the hub of a wheel, we connect to other people's heart centers, sharing energy, support, and ideas, creating a fulfilling, balanced ecosystem of heart-to-heart relationships. For the wheel to withstand rapid forward motion, the spokes need to be strong and in balance; one spoke cannot be longer or shorter than the other. This may sound idealistic, but it is possible to attain in a soul group formation. When we are off balance, we fall into a push-pull dynamic in which one person is grasping for more power and the other withdraws.

When a soul group reaches the point of harmony, it is a state of pure love. Love is all-encompassing; it is much grander than surface-level hugs, smiles, embraces, and lovemaking sessions. All those are beautiful things, but when you tap into a state of *pure love,* you enter a world that may be unlike any you can ever recall. In this world, you shine in your fullness, your soul is fully expressed, and you are embraced by all that is. On Earth, we feel separated from that divine presence. We long for it because it is possible and it is our original nature. Reconnecting with your *Monad* satisfies the longing for the perfected family. You are no longer alone, separated, or confused. It is important to stay in the center of your sphere and not cave in or lean on anyone else too hard. When you stand in the center of your sphere, and in resonance with those in your soul group, each in Vertical Alignment and fully supporting their own center, you stitch together the flower of life and magnetize your soul group. This Golden Network consists of your interwoven spheres overlapping and coming together.

Notice that the network consists of many spheres, overlapping and interwoven. Synchronicity is here to guide you to this Golden Network. This is your perfected geometric shape in the fifth dimension, awaiting your conscious awareness of its existence.

You will magnetize your soul group members when you spend time with others who also have found their central core and are self-standing, sovereign, vertically aligned, and free (or at least are actively practicing this goal). Hang out with people who have moved beyond blame and shame, each one having created his or her own radiant reality. Your shared connections in the network will flourish, and you can give and receive from your inner joy freely. Look for these types of friends, colleagues, and community members to help you establish a larger field of harmonic resonance.

Within such a soul group, creativity abounds, and there is no judgment, blame, or failure—only love and support. To bring balance to the Earth and to all people, magnetize your soul group and weave this Golden Network, which will carry us through any challenging times ahead. When people are in their center, they stop the push-pull dynamic and are able to live in harmonic resonance. They are no longer fed by the horizontal plane, but, rather, fully sustained by their vertical axis, which creates a beautifully awake and self-responsive system. If you do not know anyone who can hold this state of consciousness with you, practice alone and call your soul group in on the etheric plane. Your *Monad* is a part of your soul. You are never separated, even though on this plane you may feel disconnected. In your meditations, ask to be reconnected to your *Monad*, and explore what happens.

If you want to meet people actively practicing harmonic resonance, visit my website and sign up to be in my Inner Circle. You will be informed about the next gathering or course of study. I host many gatherings throughout the year online and in person. KnowTheSelf.com

Find the Divine Union Within

This famous symbol of two snakes winding around a pole together, twisting and turning until their heads meet at the top and their tongues kiss, is called the *caduceus*. This symbol represents the kundalini energy waking up and rising from the base of your spine. It must find its internal balance in order to fully bloom into your authentic and refined spirit expression. The two snakes represent the masculine and feminine primal energies that live within each of us. They represent the negative and positive forces, the yin and the yang, the ida and pingala.

     The goal is to make peace and find balance with the negative and positive forces inside us. When you seek peace inside yourself, these two primal forces will push, pull, and seesaw with each other to find their balance of polarity, which is experienced as an *internal* paradox. As the light quotient in your body increases, it will cast a shadow. This begins the great internal balancing act and your internal paradox of polarity will become stronger and need to express itself for you to fully understand this dynamic. The paradox is stretching your inner corridor of light—your *shushumna,* as it's referred to in Sanskrit—to be wider. The rod going up the center of the caduceus symbol represents our shushumna, which encases our physical spinal column. The central channel is the magical through line, our path to liberation and full Self-realization.

In relations with another person, the two of you will further exaggerate this zigzag effect of negative and positive patterns being pushed back and forth in order to clear out your channels and find harmonic resonance. It is the great cosmic dance as both aspects of you (also depicted by you and your partner) climb around this pole. At each turn, the negative programs you share (often the opposite pole) are mirrored back to you as you play out a push-pull dynamic. It will create an attraction and repulsion with each interaction, as depicted by the intertwined snakes. When you attract, you come together, and when you are repulsed, you push apart. As you expose, clear, and digest the negative programs, you reach more expanded levels of consciousness until you meet at the top of the staff in ultimate freedom and harmonic balance. What most people fail to recognize is that by meeting at the top in liberation, it does not negate the tail as less important than the head, nor does it negate the body of the snake. The entire path of emergence and dance between the push and pull is required to hold the awakened state of liberation that exists in the space between the two.

There is a beautiful new world awaiting you, awaiting us all. It is a world of love, support, interdependence, clarity, understanding, good will, honesty, and authenticity. It is a world of purpose, where everybody stands in their sovereign presence, knowing exactly who they are at a soul level, what they are here to give, and how we are to work together in harmonic frequency for the good of all. This is a type of cooperation that we only have witnessed in the animal kingdom, in jungles, forests, and oceans and on plains among the flora and the fauna. However, it's not reserved for the animal kingdom. *You* have the same capacity within yourself. We all do! When we attune to synchronicity and take responsibility to balance our internal paradox, we step onto the path and are able to experience the New Earth as a reality.

Understand the Twin Soul / Twin Flame Phenomena

When I first discovered that I was a Twin Soul, I assumed everybody had a twin. Over time, I have come to realize this is not the case. Instead, what has recently been revealed to me is that the majority of people on the planet right now are *Single* Souls. There is a smaller percentage of people who are *Twins,* and there are even fewer who are *Triplets*, *Quadruplets*, or even *Sextuplets*!

I have come to understand that as certain types of "older souls" increase their light quotient and evolution, they divide into multiple soul "pieces" in order to complete their mission and distribute the high intensity of energy they contain to be more effective here on Earth. Souls *divide* in order to fulfill their specific agenda and overcome the intense amnesia that happens in this dimension. They must undergo very specific challenges and initiations in order to "re-member" themselves. These particular types of twin souls emanate a strong frequency. Twins act as homing beacons and are here to assist humanity in a very specific way—through magnetization. This means twin souls will experience even more separation than a typical single soul would in order to activate their gift and find their way back to wholeness and fulfill their mission. When souls descend by multiplying themselves into more than one vehicle, they carry the power of magnetization and manifestation much more strongly than singles souls because it is their job to anchor more souls back to the *Monad*. Twin souls also carry the pain of emotional anguish and intense separation anxiety that originates from their division. Yet, they have a stronger ability to be alone for much longer periods of time than single souls.

A Twin Soul (also referred to as a twin flame) is a complete individual that was divided to hold two opposite polarities at the time of the original assignment in order to re-member and magnetize itself awake. The soul divides before the soul chooses a human form. It occurs when the soul is released from its Source.

The idea of souls being divided into multiple wholes might sound strange to you, but is similar to how identical twins are formed in the womb. However, in the nonphysical world, there is a profound experience of "oneness" and co-creation at play. I discovered this by re-experiencing my own division.

When talking about twin flames, most people romanticize this notion and really do not know what they are talking about. Many couples I have found online who call themselves "twin flames" are caught in a romantic fad that is trending in our spiritual vernacular. I feel what they are describing is more commonly either their divine complement or a soul-mate relationship.

What I have come to understand is that our twin flame is *not* our long-lost romantic partner, not in any conventional sense. The deep yearning we feel for a twin is because they are literally the other half of "us." The twin flame reunion and longing goes way beyond romance. It is actually meant to bring us together for much larger work at a galactic level where romance does not exist and only pure love is present. Twins have a mission-driven connection for humanity; a twin will slowly awaken to this in order to re-member itself. Connecting with your twin is a big part of your soul mission, but it doesn't necessarily mean you will physically work together or be romantic partners. But, if you do find yourself in physical proximity to your twin, it will be surely be powerful and very effective.

Meeting your twin soul is like taking a rocket ship to clearing your karma. It speeds up your soul's evolutionary process to the highest octave [mixed metaphor] imaginable. If you have already met your twin, it means you are ready to activate your gift and be of service in a grand way. Most twins I have met feel they are unable to handle the amount of intensity that occurs in the re-membering process. It can be agonizing when twin flames incarnate at the same time, as their vibrational frequency clears out negative programs at an extremely fast rate. Twins only incarnate at the same time in order to activate *big* change for their soul group. It is rare that this occurs in the same timeline, so you will have few past incarnations on Earth with your twin. However, when you do incarnate in the same timeline, it is because you are needed to serve your soul group in a larger capacity. Incarnating together happens during grand cycles. It looks and feels quite dramatic and is most often very painful for the two individuals, along with everyone else in the dynamic with them including their family, friends, and people in their vicinity. It is a magnificent ride when twins meet, and the sooner the twins learn how to clear, heal, and deepen the roots of their personal star seed, the faster they will evolve and transcend the challenges it will surely present.

Standing in the presence of your twin soul will vibrate and activate your star seed to find its larger *Monadic* match. Imagine two magnets with extreme polarity. If you put your hand between twins, the magnetic pull is immense; the power between them is palpable. When your twin is not in human form, you will still feel its presence in your meditations, dreams, and waking life as a guardian angel and loving assistant. If you are a twin, the majority of your lifetimes will be with one of you helping from another plane of existence to keep you on your path.

If you are wondering whether you are a twin soul, understand that this is not a romantic fairy tale; it is made in our spiritual anatomy, just like we don't walk around assuming we might have an identical twin sibling when we were born as a single entity. If you were not born as a twin sibling, you would not walk around pretending you were, right? That would be strange. But many people are doing exactly this because they have read the term somewhere and have misunderstood what it means. Being a twin soul and meeting yours in this dimension is the groundwork of a very difficult and demanding relationship. If you are wondering whether "so and so" is your twin flame, meditate deeply on the notion and track where the question is coming from. Is this because you heard about twins somewhere, or is it from a deep inner knowing? Ask for guidance from your soul, look for the signs before jumping to any conclusions or declaring your twin status in public. There are many twins incarnating together now because of the great turning we are experiencing.

The awareness of being a twin comes to one person first, but both twins will come to the understanding of their own accord. Neither I nor my twin had any idea there was such a concept as *twin soul*. Neither of us had ever heard of it, we never discussed it, and to top it off, he is a very skeptical person and not interested in spiritual beliefs whatsoever. Even so, we both came to know we were twin souls in our own way. I remember the day we discussed it, but first I will explain how I realized we were twins.

Our relationship was emotionally unbearable from the instant we spoke. The feelings we were having toward each other were intense and destabilizing for both of us. It was at once confusing and exciting. Being in each other's presence was mesmerizing. We would stare into each other's eyes without speaking for long periods of time and know exactly what the other was thinking. We would enter into a kind of hypnotic state. When we were apart, I could sense his feelings at all times. Whenever I wanted to, I could have long conversations with him in my head, and he would respond! We would later speak and confirm these strong feelings of inner knowing. We were both aware of this magical ability we so palpably had with each other. It was a level of trust I had never experienced before. Our emotions for each other were off the charts, and neither of us could control our expression of these big feelings, which never seemed appropriate. Our relationship felt scary, for he was a married man, and our relationship started out as purely a business friendship. I felt out of control in his presence. I was never sure what was going to happen, as we had a strange ability to peer into each other's soul. It was the most vulnerable either of us had ever felt in the presence of another.

I decided to undergo a past life regression session with my friend Monish in Hyderabad to find some resolve. Since meeting my twin, I had multiple visions of how I knew him in other lifetimes. I wanted Monish to regress me to one of the lifetimes in which we must have endured a great hardship. I needed to heal the intense feeling I was experiencing. Before the session with Monish, I had experienced multiple regression sessions over the years in my own meditations and with various practitioners, so regressions were a common experience for me. However, what transpired in my work with Monish was unlike any other past life session.

It started out as they normally do. I went to one timeline story and re-lived that life, but my strong emotions didn't feel resolved. Then, Monish sent me back further in time to find the *original wound* that held the pain of this relationship. What I experienced was my original descent from source. My twin and I were exact polar opposites and literally pulled apart and split into two human forms! It was an Adam and Eve experience. It was excruciating to my physical and emotional body to re-live this memory, as it felt like my spine was being split into two. During the session, I flopped around on the floor and cried out in agony as I re-experienced that soul memory. After that extremely cathartic and challenging session, it all made perfect sense to my soul knowing, but it took many years for my mind to grasp the meaning of what I saw. The deep longing, the psychic connection, the role we were here to play, and the reason we needed to split was all shown to me in a stream of images that flickered through my mind's eye like a movie.

I was reluctant to share my experience with my twin because he wasn't interested in past life regressions or spiritual philosophy. He is a very practical person who shuns religion and spiritual pursuits. Still, as I began to tell him what I saw, he explained to me that he already knew all of it. He himself had experienced a few dreams and had come to some deep understandings in his own way about our soul connection. He hadn't told me because he was unable to put words to it. When we shared our experiences with each other, we were further convinced that these were not random dreams and visions but actual truth.

I have interviewed other twins with similar stories. What I've heard in common with all of them is that the *knowing* was always a time-released unfolding for how each twin remembered; it always came as a surprise. Both twins would have a profound dream, a paranormal experience, or some sort of direct realization. It was never a guessing game or something they learned from a website. So if you are guessing about someone being your twin, that person is most likely *not* your twin flame.

Twin flames meeting in the physical plane do not need to engage in a romantic relationship; in fact, most of the time twins cannot sustain romance because of the drama involved. However, the first inclination in meeting your twin will be to make it romantic because of the deep yearning you will feel for the other half of your soul. Romantic attachments are a trap that binds us to this three-dimensional plane of existence. Our twin is appearing in our life to activate the other planes of existence and restore us to wholeness. Remember, we live in a multidimensional universe, and while twin flames can create intense romantic feelings such as deep longing for the other, those longings are not romantic in nature. Rather, they come from the longing you both share to return to your *Monadic* Source. If you are seeking your twin flame or have found yours and are struggling to keep them close, know that the romantic notions are a complete and total *trap of samskaras (karmic ties).* This dynamic duo needs a lot of personal space. If you fall into a romantic haze, it will keep you in a push-pull dynamic for a very long time and in an extreme way that is often painful yet necessary to learn the skills to transcend it. The polarities of twin flames are complete opposites, though on the other side of their karmic clearing, when they find their sovereignty, they can activate a harmonic resonance, a perfected balanced state of the highest order, as the caduceus symbolizes. As a result, when you and your twin can cooperate, heal, and expand your consciousness together and steer clear of drama, you will be delivering an invaluable gift to everyone on the planet.

When you meet your twin, you will have an intense psychic capacity to communicate with each other telepathically, oftentimes for years before you ever meet in physical form. You will feel more intimate and experience more love with your twin than with anyone you have ever loved before. It will feel like the completion of the other half of your soul because that is exactly what it is. This reunion is needed for a complete remembering of your soul essence.

Your duty to your twin is to clear your past karma and negative patterns on your own. You are coming together to speed up your healing and to create an alliance for the planet's evolution while burning through your own personal karma along the way. If you are lucky (and have a lighter karmic load), you may enjoy romance, too. But do not let romance be your primary attachment to your twin flame, as it is much bigger than that and it will hold you in a hostage pattern of self-destruction. One of you will recognize the self-sabotage and run away; the other will chase the runner. It is a destructive pattern until one of the twins decides to do the work to evolve. When one twin evolves, the other evolves naturally.

As you come together with your twin flame, a lot of friction and polarity will get kicked up around you and out to your entire soul group. As you come into balance within yourself, at a soul level you are restructuring the grid to which you are all connected. The more you practice holding your own sovereignty and being responsible for your field (your circle), the more you activate your *Monad* and magnetize the soul group back together. Such ripples are felt throughout the golden latticework that holds every soul in your group together. This harmonic resonance is like a homing device, calling your soul group to return home.

When twin flames are fully activated in harmonic balance, their vibration increases in power, and they have the ability to activate their entire soul group. In my meditations, I have seen that when one soul group of twelve activates, the entire *Monad* of 144,000 will automatically activate through a cascading event. Twin souls are drawn to pair up and create a harmonic resonance so they can be fused back together into oneness. This fusing opens the gate to the New Earth. When this occurs, the twins will invert. Instead of being polarized face-to-face, they will be magnetized back-to-back and in an entirely new dimensional form, as One.

Your twin flame and your divine complement may not be in human form at this moment. He or she may appear more as a guardian angel, or a spirit that walks with you, so to speak. Even if your twin flame is not alive on the planet at this time, it will feel like they can project their spirit and walk alongside of you if you both will it to be. This is an important time to energetically reunite with the other eleven people of your soul group. As you link up with these souls, synchronicity abounds, and you awaken to your divine nature. Together, you become like human keys able to access the *New Earth* reality that brings us—all of us— into powerful harmonic resonance, thus leading us to reach our full potential as multidimensional humans.

* * *

Romance is beautiful, fun, and enlivening, but it is a fleeting feeling that we cannot hold on to or control. The moment we do, we find it escapes us. Many of us get caught riding a romantic wave and become addicted to the thrill of the chase and the capture. We leap like frogs from lily pad to lily pad, hoping we won't ever have to swim or dive. While lily pads are wonderful platforms from which beautiful flowers emerge, like synchronicity, they are just the images and symbols to illumine one's path. And, as with lily pads, when you stay on the surface, you miss the depths. It is important to honor the deep roots that grew in the dark, swampy waters, which nourish the beautiful lotus flower.

There is a multi-dimensional nature to relationships that you will miss if you stick to the surface level, clinging solely to romance and staying stuck in a push-pull dynamic. Step out of the matrix and the old program of romance and dig deeper by reaching for something higher. In other words, stay vertical.

Remember the Greek caduceus symbol, which is often used in the medical industry, as a metaphor for your romantic partnership. The legend of this symbol is that Hermes used his staff to separate two fighting snakes; they intertwined around it and remained in balanced harmony (depicted by the wings at the top).

I see this symbol as a mirror for our relationships. The snakes' movement from the lower, denser chakras up and into the higher chakras represents the move from our own base physical desires to the connected wings of Spirit.

In this new light, you shine in your full potential and are embraced by *All-That-Is*. Unconditional love, when experienced, is the feeling of finally arriving home to yourself. There is a large congregation waiting to receive you, nourish you, love you, and celebrate you. The Monad sees your beauty, your genius, and your unique light. Unconditional love is the feeling we spend all our lives longing for.

Key #6
Be Happy for No Reason

"The most valuable possession you can own is an open heart. The most powerful weapon you can be is an instrument of peace."
— Carlos Santana

Sometimes, the messy environment in which you find yourself is actually in your mind. It is your thoughts that are creating a huge electromagnetic storm inside your own head. When this happens, it is important to remember that you can control the weather inside your head.

We tend to think that our thoughts are a part of us, created by us. Some thoughts may be so habituated that they have been running on instant replay for most of your life, never to be questioned. The truth is that your thoughts are simply electrical triggers; they are not *who you are*. By choosing to have different thoughts, you can literally switch off one electrical circuit and switch on another in your brain. When you do this, you create a new, positive circuit that can rewire your thoughts, which, in turn, changes the electrical patterns in your mind.

Since your thoughts are what trigger your emotions, by creating new thoughts, you can create new emotions and, therefore, break out of negative patterns that keep you stuck. This may sound too simple to be true if you are a pessimist, but even so, I invite you to commit for at least 21 days to a daily practice of rewiring your thoughts. It's not only possible to do, it's enjoyable. The hard part is staying vigilant about what you are telling yourself all day that is keeping you sad, angry, or frustrated. Generally, it is the critical parent hiding out in your psyche that keeps you feeling small and victimized. This critical parent needs to be highlighted inside your psyche in order to be re-patterned into a caring, loving, and compassionate voice.

Let me give you an example from my own experience. For much of my life, I found myself feeling unsafe and victimized wherever I went. I have experienced all kinds of dramatic encounters like sexual harassment, rape, being held at knifepoint on multiple occasions—I even escaped a bullet by seconds. I found myself in dangerous environments far too often. I had a program running that I was a human target and that my life was a scary and unsafe place to be. When I got tired of playing the victim and decided I, as the creator of my reality, could shift this experience, I dug deep into my psyche to see where that belief lived and how it had been playing out in my experience. I realized my childhood abuse had created a soul wound that caused the cycle to repeat. It was hard wired in my energetic field and attracted those situations to me time and again. Realizing I could be at cause in my life, I chose to install a new thought pattern that would give me different experiences. It required analyzing all the choices I made and consciously choosing friends, situations, and places that evoked safety. I know this sounds obvious, but it wasn't at the time. I didn't realize all the sneaky ways that pattern played out unconsciously.

Do you tend to be pessimistic about your life? Maybe you are someone who finds a lot of things wrong before you see the good? Look back at the previous few days. How happy were you? If you have a lot to complain about, or you feel that life could be, or should be, so much better, then I want to share with you a few steps that will leave you feeling happy for no reason.

Numerous studies show that people who are open and optimistic about life have a stronger immune system and bounce back quicker after upsets. Happiness and positivity are key to optimal health and wellness, but many people don't know how to be happy. If you suffer from the "grass is greener" mindset, then listen up. The answer to your happiness lives within you, and I'm going to show you how easy it is to create a powerful mind shift to make a change for the better.

Feel Your Ideals

How much love can you handle? Are you really ready for your prayers to be answered? I ask you this because I wasn't ready. I didn't know how to open up to this type of pure love, and I see this with many of my students as well. For many years, I was praying for something I was not able to receive. I prayed for peace in my family without even knowing what it might feel like. I prayed for unconditional love from my partner without having a clue of what that meant. I prayed for honesty and authenticity without first experiencing it within myself.

Here's the thing—the Universe can't give you something you don't make space for. Whatever your deep longing is, make sure you know how to receive it!

* * *

In the following exercise, I'll share a simple tool for getting unstuck, magnetizing your attraction channels, and staying in the flow toward your divine destiny. This exercise will make space in your life for miracles to appear. It helped me transform my life in countless ways. I have been using this practice for over 20 years in every area of my life, and it truly works.

Are you ready? This doesn't take long, but it takes focus and purity of heart. Allow yourself time for the entire process. Track it for a few weeks or a few months, and you will begin to see miraculous results. I call this exercise *Positive Vibrational Repatterning* because you need to fully vibrate the positive vibes you want to call toward you in order to repattern yourself for it and manifest it in your reality. In time, you will learn to trust this process to open to it fully, becoming a master manifestor. Are you ready? Here we go!

Positive Vibrational Repatterning

Take out your journal and write your answers to the following questions:

1. What is it that you truly want to experience in your life? What do you long for from the bottom of your heart?

2. Close your eyes and imagine that you are experiencing it right now. What does it feel like in your body to have that desire as a reality? Feel into the sensation of having it be true in this moment.

3. Write down at least six feelings of how it felt to experience that desire being met.

4. What would need to change in your life to experience that reality? What would need to be different?

5. Who would you have to be in order to experience that reality?

6. What steps are you willing to take toward making this reality possible?

7. What do you need to sacrifice or give up in order to have this reality?

In order to loosen the grip of our negative thoughts, we need to balance them out with positive *feelings* to align ourselves with having more positive experiences. You can download my Positive Vibrational Repatterning worksheet on my website to guide you even deeper into this exercise: KnowTheSelf.com/workbook.

Understand Right Use of Will

When your star seed takes root, new energy circuits will awaken in your light body and your intuition, and other ways of seeing will start to develop. You will quickly find yourself harnessing new power, the power of your soul's knowing. It is important to make sure you are using your newfound power responsibly. At first, you may make a lot of mistakes, though hopefully not too many. There are a few protocols to keep in mind when exercising your newfound abilities.

To start with, make sure you always examine your motives to ensure your intention for using your innate gifts is directed from a clear heart. If there is anything you are trying to gain personally, you simply need to acknowledge it and release any attachment to it. Offer your gift as a vehicle of service and make sure you are in service to the higher order of a *win-win*, not your own selfish desires, and you will transcend your lower programs. The misuse of your energy will ricochet back to harm you, so it is imperative to keep your heart and motives clear.

There are ways of acting out that can create tears in this beautiful golden latticework that the spiritual warriors are working so hard to re-stitch. Participating in gossip, having bad intentions, and lustfulness, greed, and corruption all damage the tapestry. These behaviors literally destroy your golden latticework. If you do participate in these behaviors, your alignment distorts and twists upon itself. When this happens, as many of us learn the hard way, do your best to clear any false or selfish motives, practice radical honesty, come back into Vertical Alignment, and clear your space of the negative imprints.

You will make mistakes as you learn how to hold this new energy; we all do. Knowing how to get unstuck and learning from your mistakes is what's critical.

When you activate your heart frequency in proper alignment, you become a resonator. As a resonator, you are able to tune yourself like a frequency beacon radio channel and project a vibrational sound wave from your morphogenetic field. By doing this, you will be able to activate others and hold your position in the latticework, which is required for strong connections to enable your soul group to reunite.

To fully attune yourself to your innate gifts, you will need to let go of the fears you were latching on to that you thought were keeping you safe. At first, this detachment from your fears will be very uncomfortable; it requires courage and a brave heart. Eventually, you will learn to become the center of your own universe and surmount your previous fears. When you learn to operate from the center of your being, you become free. You will be a joy to behold, and your presence will be a gift to everyone with whom you come into contact.

To keep your frequency in balance, practice these steps:

- **Choose Your Company Carefully.** Like a tuning fork when struck, being in close proximity to those who are tuned to their own center will take you to your center the fastest. The opposite is also true. So, socialize and meditate with people who are calm, poised, and centered, if that is the frequency you most desire. Remember, we become like those with whom we spend most of our time.

- **Set an Intention.** Hold a clear intention and a deep desire to feel into the center of your being and align with the flow of synchronicity. Take mini meditation breaks throughout the day. Even simple conscious-breathing exercises (counting to ten breaths or more) can work miracles!

- **Motive Check.** Identify what you are being driven by. Is it lust, greed, or power? If so, step back and readjust your intention. Too often, people are driven by the unconscious programs of lust, greed, and power, but when we bring our honest attention to the things we want, we can often expose these lower programs and let them go before it's too late.

As we harmonize with the natural world, we become more in tune with the Universal Laws that govern our life. The Law of Cause and Effect is always at play. In order to keep yourself in good karmic standing, it's important to attune to your center and practice the right use of your willpower. Otherwise, you are just causing more suffering for others and yourself. Your intentions need to be checked on a regular basis in order to know your true nature. Thoughts (unconscious or not) create your reality. Keeping a sharp eye on your personal motivations will help you keep your scales in balance.

Guidelines for Harmonic Resonance

As you embark on your path of self-discovery, your life will change rapidly. It can be confusing to navigate a changing reality.

Here's a list of guidelines for how to conduct yourself that I request all of my students (and myself) to follow in order to hold harmony, within and without:

- Be here in the now, physically and emotionally, as you work with the material in this book and awaken to your innate genius. Have no regrets for yesterday. Life is in you today, and you are making your tomorrows.
- Accept yourself exactly where you are and as you are.
- Be open to others being exactly where they are. Take responsibility only for yourself.
- As you alter your relationship with yourself, your external world will alter accordingly. Your

way of speaking and dressing may change. Allow that to happen and simply witness it.

- Be curious about and compassionate with yourself in this deeply transformative process.
- When you start to take responsibility and start to see yourself as the source of your experience, do so from a place of profound self-acceptance, healthy curiosity, and a very impersonal position. Relate to your own experience from a perspective of being collectively part of the human experience, rather than shaming, blaming, or considering yourself wrong.
- Be open and ready to change, noticing any resistance that comes up that needs to be cleared away.
- Allow others to have their own processes and personal space.
- Make "I" statements when speaking about your experience. Own your feelings and take responsibility for them through your language.
- Do not speak negatively of yourself or others. Don't discredit yourself or minimize your abilities.
- Don't compromise your own reality.
- Be your own advisor, keep your own counsel, and make your own decisions.
- Be compassionate with others, but true to your own goals.
- If you fall short of your ethics, acknowledge it, make up for the damage done, communicate with anyone with whom you need to make amends, and move on.

- Activate your empathic listening from Source rather than ego or judgment (hear others as God hears them). As people connect with you, give them undivided love, light, and energy. Shower them with light, and imagine them communicating clearly and effectively.
- Be aware of how you are showing up in your social life and of your need to share or your hesitation to share.
- If you're sharing about what has happened in your life, share from your own experience. Share what happened to you, rather than gossiping or adding judgment.
- Speak directly to others when you have a concern. No gossiping.
- Respect confidentiality. What happens during deep intimacy stays close to your heart.

Do you want to practice these guidelines in a group harmonic field with me? If so, you can join one of my group offerings and receive training and support on activating your star seed, strengthening your integrity, and magnetizing your soul group. For more information, visit my website, KnowTheSelf.com.

Flex Your Gratitude Muscle

The feeling of being happy (or simply being at peace with yourself) is connected to feelings of gratitude. Gratitude can be practiced and exercised, just like a muscle. The more you consciously conjure up feelings of gratitude, the brighter your outlook becomes. When you begin to exercise your gratitude muscle, you will learn how to open yourself to the blessings life brings, no matter what the situation may be.

This technique is so simple that many people are reluctant to try it, thinking anything this easy cannot possible work. However, the proof is in the results. Try it to understand how effective it is.

Begin exercising your gratitude muscle throughout your day, and watch the Universe pour its blessings upon you. It's easy, and it works. You can download this handy Emotional Guidance Scale to help you out with this exercise at: KnowTheSelf.com/workbook.

Here are the five basic steps:

1. **Listen to what you tell yourself all day long.** What type of commentary fills the empty spaces in your mind? If you are not sure, look at yourself in the mirror and you will hear that voice start to chatter. Or simply sit quietly and listen to the thoughts that keep recurring in the background.

2. **Choose to change the channel.** Many people have been operating on autopilot their whole lives, not realizing they have the power to choose what to think about. When you hear those negative, subconscious tapes

running, decide to think about something positive.

3. **Find something to be grateful for.** It could be as simple as a pretty flower, or the smile of a young person. No matter how bad things seem, there is *always* something beautiful within reach for which to be grateful.

4. **Design a set of positive power statements for yourself.** Neurolinguistic programming is a simple science that yields extraordinary results. Feed yourself some positive power statements every time you look in the mirror, and notice how it begins to shift your reality. See the power statement examples below to get you going, or create your own.

5. **Trust in the process, and give it a chance.** Decide to implement this new healthy habit for the next 30 days. You could find a buddy to exercise your gratitude muscle and positive power statements with, too. This process is a soothing balm to the soul and a gift to your spirit.

Here are some power statements to get you in the flow of being grateful:

- All of life loves and supports me.
- I am surrounded by love everywhere I go.

- My mere existence inspires my partner beyond his/her wildest imagination.
- What was my pain is now my power.
- I listen with love to my body's messages.
- Loving others is easy when I love and accept myself.
- I am flexible and flowing.
- I prosper wherever I turn.
- My thoughts are creative.
- I forgive myself.

What did you notice when you flexed your gratitude muscle? Send me an email and tell me about it: info@knowtheself.com. Let's make the world a better place, together, one thought at a time!

Are You Moving Forward or Backward?

As you embark on the journey of knowing your true Self, you will likely encounter setbacks, drama, trauma, and debilitating mindsets. How do you stay the course? How do you know you are moving forward and not backward?

It is easy to fall back into despair after climbing out of an emotional rut only to find yourself, again and again, unconsciously repeating the same saga with new people, new places, and new situations but with the same crummy feeling.

Tracking internal growth can be tricky. Inner shifts are often subtle and intangible. Do not dismay! There is an easy way to know if you are progressing along your soulful journey. The thing to remember is that we grow in spirals, moving up to higher levels of consciousness. These spirals, however, often feel like never-ending circles.

How do you know you are growing spiritually and not cycling in stagnancy? I used to feel frustrated with my own spiritual evolution and personal growth, until I learned how to track this invisible kind of progress. It seemed that just as I believed I had overcome an old pattern, I found myself repeating it. My old patterns seemed to become smarter and lurk in my blind spots only to re-emerge when I least suspected it, causing me much frustration and, often, deep despair—until I learned how to track my invisible progress.

I began to use the four stages of growth, which I outline below, as guideposts to track myself as I transformed through the inner journey of discovering my true Self. I first heard of these four stages from listening to a talk by Lisa Nichols, a powerful motivational speaker. I diligently took notes as she shared her personal discovery. Then, I began mapping it in my own life. Here is how I have come to understand these four stages for myself. I hope you find it as useful as I do.

Stage One starts when you decide to take responsibility for the actions, thoughts, and ways of being that are attracting negative patterns in your life. By identifying what you do that keeps the negative pattern in place, you have reached the first stage. Once you accept your responsibility and make the pattern conscious, you are well on your way to shifting it. Denial has lost its grip!

Stage Two starts after you've identified the offending thought, action, or habit that keeps you stuck. You will begin to notice all the times you continue to act this out. Stage two is a difficult stage because you feel like you can't help but stay trapped in this cycle. You begin to see how ingrained it is in your psyche, unconsciously acting out without thought. It will continue happening (like it has been before), only in stage two. you are aware of how much you do it.

This is the stage where many people remain stuck. You might wish you could go back to how ignorant you were before you became so hyper aware of yourself. But don't give up! At this stage, you are well on your way to changing the habit or cycle that is entrapping you. Keep your eyes open, and notice all the ways this pattern runs your life. Cultivate compassion and forgiveness toward yourself, and you will succeed in moving to the next stage.

Stage Three happens when you know you have passed the discomfort of Stage Two and you become aware that you are about to repeat that offending pattern or habit. However, this time, just before you do it, you pause and decide to do something positive instead. Congratulations! This is the time to celebrate. Your awareness has expanded. You have just overcome a huge hurdle. You have restored your choice and personal power to create change.

Stage Four is a godsend on this seemingly never-ending wheel of repeating patterns. What is funny about stage four is that as the final stage, it shows up so easily you may forget you worked so hard to get here. It happens when you no longer have to anticipate your old negative way of being because you have a positive new response that happens automatically. When you reach this stage, you know you have moved fully beyond your old negative pattern. Celebrate your newfound freedom, and keep up the great work!

I asked my dear friend and conscious collaborator, Nomita, to design a diagram of these four stages so we all can be reminded of them and refer to the diagram when we feel discouraged or depressed about our efforts. Overcoming negative patterning is a process, and, as such, it requires patience.

I highly recommend you download this handy diagram. Print it out and keep it next to your personal re-charge station so you can refer to it on challenging days: KnowTheSelf.com/workbook.

"What was my pain, is now my power." 4.

You have fully succeeded in installing a new positive pattern. Your old pattern no longer has a hold on you. Your true self is being revealed.

3.

"Whoa, almost did it again...(but I didn't)!"

Congratulations! You've just learned how to restore choice and take back your power.

2.

"I juuust did it, again!"

Noticing all the ways in which you sabotage yourself is very uncomfortable. Hang in there, you are beginning to peel off the layers of old conditioning. Your true Self is being unveiled.

1.

"Do I really do that?"

You have just overcome denial. Change is well on its way.

4 Stages of Inner Growth

A tracking system to overcome mental, emotional, spiritual and physical addictions.

© amelia | www.KnowTheSelf.com

These four stages of growth can be applied to any internal growth cycle, whether you are overcoming an addiction, a bad habit, or a negative attraction. Refer to these stages whenever you are in doubt or feeling like your internal journey is becoming too challenging. Cultivating trust and faith in your process of inner transformation will help you move through the cycles quicker. Use the graphic for a handy reference.

Isn't it satisfying to know you can change? You may feel unworthy of what your soul presents as a path forward, or you might feel guilty or selfish as you move toward your ideals. In those moments, it is imperative that you find a mentor, an elder, or a coach who can guide you and provide the support you need to develop your strength to follow through and face your fears. Everyone deserves to be happy and liberated.

Where do you get stuck on your journey? I'd love to hear from you. If you would like personal assistance with your inner transformation, please reach out: info@KnowTheSelf.com.

Key #7
Walk the Path of Healing

"I must not fear. Fear is the mind-killer. Fear is the little-death that brings total obliteration. I will face my fear. I will permit it to pass over me and through me. And when it has gone past I will turn the inner eye to see its path. Where the fear has gone there will be nothing. Only I will remain."
– Frank Herbert, Dune

As you awaken to higher states of consciousness, your nervous system will need support to stay steady and relaxed. Your system will go through several spikes as your body opens to your star seed and learns to adapt to this new form of pure energy. This can be an uncomfortable phase of the awakening process. Stabilizing the body's energy becomes a primary need.

When you begin to meditate and do the Vertical Alignment exercise, you will notice that your entire physical body will go through subtle changes. At first, you might notice it in your speech patterns. Simple preferences might change, like the way you dress or the type of food you eat. You may even realize you've started attracting different types of people into your life.

Your friends might change, and you may feel out of place in your relationships and need to adjust them.

At a physical level, you will also experience changes. You might wake up and look totally renewed. People might comment on your glow or tell you that you look different, or they might not recognize you at all. You might quickly lose weight and muscle mass, or become strong and lean in a short period of time.

Strange electrical sensations may occur in your brain as new neurons begin pinging back and forth and opening up formerly closed neural pathways. You might find your body jerking around or spontaneously shaking in reaction to energy spikes shooting up your spine. You might find yourself itching like crazy for a few moments on the top of your head as the energy awakens. When this happens, go with it. Do not fight it, and do not exaggerate it. Just allow it to move and push through the blockages.

In heightened energetic times, you may find you have no need for sleep or food. On the other hand, you may need to sleep for days or eat a lot more as your body heats up.

Specific chakras (energy centers) along the front of your spine may begin to throb or pulsate when activated. Your heart, when learning to contain more love, may feel like it's under a ton of pressure as it stretches open.

These are all normal symptoms of the star seed awakening process. The most important thing is to ground your system regularly and hold Vertical Alignment. Refer to the exercises in Key #3 and Key #4 to hone your energy patterns and find your inner balance.

When you awaken this star seed in your heart center, it can feel like an explosion as it instantly dispels false beliefs and leaves you in pieces, trying to make sense of what just happened. The old programs need to fall away for your original blueprint to take its place.

Course corrections are part of the natural cycle of nature needing to save itself. Think of them as internal earthquakes demanding your attention to re-pattern. When you feel like you are in pieces and need to pull yourself back together, refer to Key #5 and Key #6, do the Positive Vibrational Repatterning Technique, practice gratitude, and use the Four Stages of Inner Growth to track your progress.

Once you have stepped onto the path of awakening your star seed, you cannot stop the process. You can try, and you will try, but you will only cause yourself inner conflict. Make sure you ask for support, as this process can drag on for quite a while depending on what work you are being prepared for. If your spiritual mission requires a lot of precision, your system will have to be completely scrubbed clean of old programs. Allow this clearing to take place, and ask for help; you will need it.

There are a number of alternative healers I call on in challenging times. My personal favorite support network consists of therapists practicing massage, Network Spinal Analysis (Network Chiropractic), cranial sacral, osteopathy, naturopathy, Ayurveda, and Chinese medicine/acupuncture, as well as shamans, astrologists, yogis, and various types of seers. It's also important to receive nutritional support and to commune with nature, including restorative trips to the closest hot springs. Whatever soothes your nervous system, relaxes your body, opens your channels, and keeps you feeling grounded will assist you.

Designate Your Counsel

Stabilizing your Vertical Alignment and healing your soul wounds are required on this journey toward wholeness. When you are flowing in the river of life, you do not need to expend as much effort. Simple prayers are heard. At the same time, when you need support, feel lost, or become exhausted from the stretching and expanding, make sure you have a wise counsel to turn to.

Said counsel can be in the form of a mentor, a trusted friend, a coach, a therapist, or whomever supports your growth. Who do you have in your life who could support you in this way?

Take a moment to grab your journal and answer the following questions:

1. Who are the people in your life who, when you are with them, help you feel safe, at home, respected, and wanted?

2. Who can you always rely on to be honest with you? This is a friend who is not afraid to tell you hard truths.

3. Which elders in your life can you rely on to greet you with open arms, listen to your problems, and give you sound advice?

4. Who among your circle of friends is the most loyal and truthful?

5. Who are the healers or therapists, or what are the therapies, that help you most?

6. Who are your mentors?

7. What communities, groups, or organizations do you belong to that give you a sense of community?

8. What people do you serve? To whom are you in service? This could include volunteer work, individuals, or organizations to which you actively contribute.

You may not have answers for some of these questions. That is okay. Now is the time to identify the voids and begin building your own wise counsel to support your conscious evolution. These are people with whom you feel an instant connection, people to whom you can turn when the going gets tough. Make a list now so that later, when you are experiencing fear and doubt along your journey, you have a list to refer to and can reach out for support.

Welcome Love as the Great Healer

Sometimes you may bully yourself, believing you are not good enough to be happy. You may punish yourself, feel ashamed of something you have done, or feel guilty about choices you have made. The eyes of the critical parent that lives in your psyche may remind you of your own mother or father judging and condemning you. This constant barrage of feelings that you're not good enough, didn't do it right, should be ashamed of yourself, are not worthy—whatever negative patterns you were taught as a child—mean that it is time to become the loving parent and choose to bring love and childlike innocence and play back into your life.

It is important to increase beauty, joy, and love in order to crowd out negative feelings. Positive vibrations instantly override lower patterns that try to take hold, convolute, corrupt, and govern your life. Love is the ultimate healer. Love overcomes all fear.

As you embark on your path of healing, it is important to accept what is and make the most of it. Even when it's painful—especially when it's painful! Track your feelings long enough to see them as patterns. You may find it helpful to liken your feelings to weather patterns. You can choose the type of "weather" you want by the thoughts you think. If you are repeating a negative thought, you are creating a negative weather pattern in your emotions. If you decide you hate Mondays or you hate traffic or you hate people near you, then every time you are faced with Mondays, or traffic, or people near you, you will have a feeling of resentment, agitation, and discomfort in your body. This causes toxins to flood your system and attract all kinds of harmful vibes. If you choose to look at the things you hate through the lens of love, you will be able to see the beauty in them. You can restore compassion and feel better instantly.

For example, let's look at your relationship with time. Do you stress yourself out all day thinking there is never enough time? Do you chase time with your anxiety or run behind it feeling fearful of it? What would happen if you could simply accept where you are in this moment and slow your breath down to become totally present? It is amazing how much time you have when you slow down and take deep breaths. It's as if time expands when you enjoy what you are doing. Joy is the key to slowing down time. Enjoy yourself. Smile. Learn how to enjoy every moment while you are in it; otherwise, you will have regrets. Instead, allow the river of life to carry you forward.

When you find yourself stressed out or anxious, stop. Take a deep breath and figure out how to smile and make whatever you are doing into a dance, or find a way to play with it, and you will learn to magically expand time. Your stress and anxiety will melt away, and you will begin to love your life.

Slow down long enough to catch the river, to enjoy and attune to what is about to unfold, what is trying to unfold, what is trying to find you. When we live in harmony at our deepest level, all things begin to resonate. We instantly heal. We instantly come back into balance.

Reclaim Prayer

Do you pray? Many of us have forgotten how to pray. Prayer is the quickest way to shift into the flow of synchronicity. We are praying all day long, whether we are aware of it or not. Our thoughts are constantly sending signals to our environment. Normally, many of the thoughts in our mind are completely subconscious and on autopilot. Reclaim your thoughts, form them into intentions, and—voíla—you are praying consciously.

Let's be honest, praying out loud can seem strange if this is new to you. Organized religion has attempted to own and govern our prayers for centuries. It is time we reclaim prayer for ourselves regardless of our religious or spiritual beliefs. Find your own form of prayer. It can be something you learned as a child or picked up somewhere along your path, but I encourage you to find a new way to pray. *Find your own authentic way to pray.*

Things won't always go your way. In fact, if you are flowing with life, your old programs will be challenged—a lot. Listen to your heart's deepest longing. What is it needing? This longing is a prayer. Allow your deep longing for your ideal to become conscious. You may not want to share that longing because that may feel too vulnerable, too deep, or too exposed. However, your longing is exactly what needs to be exposed. Speak it out loud, write it down, and share it as a prayer.

The deep longing is what awakens your star seed. It awakens your sacred heart and allows the river of life to pick you up and carry you home to your divine destiny. If you dare to share your deep longing, you will begin to magnetize it. The more you imagine it as already present, the sooner you will be able to fully receive it. Pray like you mean it, and activate your ability to co-create. There is no reason to play small and live at the level of effect when you can consciously live at the level of cause in your life.

Call in the Light

In India, mantras (translated from Sanskrit as "sacred syllables" or "instruments of thought") are used to invoke energy and to heal impurities of the mind, body, and spirit. Mantras are vibrational formulas that were perfectly designed, thousands of years ago, to produce geometric patterns with their precise pronunciation and intonations. These ancient sound formulas are a powerful form of prayer and devotion that can be used for achieving your ideal.

You have probably heard the most popular mantra, "Om" or "Aum." This magical syllable (depicted in Sanskrit above), when intoned, evokes the divine spark within. It is the cosmic sound, the seed sound from which all life sprung. Intone the mantra sound "Om" and allow the vibration to recalibrate your heart and mind. It will bring all your energy centers into alignment. If you don't want to say or sing it out loud, simply think upon it and it will have the same effect.

Mantras invoke powerful vibrational force when we listen to them, sing them, speak them, or think them. There are thousands of mantras in the ancient Hindu texts. Those mantras were created for every kind of situation or illness imaginable. There is one mantra in particular that I find the most helpful when I am face to face with darkness. It is called the Gayatri Mantra (see below). It is very popular in India and primarily sung at sunrise and sunset as a spiritual devotion to keep the light alive. Anytime you feel darkness, remember that singing, saying, or listening to this mantra will instantly bring back the light of a thousand suns. Listen to this mantra and discover how you feel. Visit my website to find a recording of this chant. I suggest memorizing it and seeing how it works for you. KnowTheSelf.com/workbook.

The Gayatri Mantra:
>Om Buhr, Bhuva, Swaha
>Om Tat Savitur Varenyam
>Bhargo Devasya Dheemahi
>Dhiyo Yonaha Prachodayat

The English translation:
>We meditate on the glory of the Creator;
>Who has created the Universe;
>Who is worthy of Worship;
>Who is the embodiment of Knowledge and Light;
>Who is the remover of Sin and Ignorance;

May He open our hearts and enlighten our Intellect.

Find a mantra or prayer that works for you. It can be from your own spiritual lineage or one to which you feel drawn. It doesn't matter where it originates. What matters is that your heart learns to open and express the deep soulful longing it holds.

Prayer is something we can reclaim. Life is full of pain and suffering until we find the light, and prayer leads us to that light.

The journey toward your divine destiny is preparing you for the New Earth. Find the tools that work for you to balance, heal, and awaken your heart. There is no right or wrong, or good or bad. Try things out; use them to see what happens. Figure out what works for you.

Discover Your Energy Flows

In our day-to-day reality, we have a lot of things to do, people to see, and places to go. How do we know which efforts are truly good for our development and which efforts are simply exhausting us and draining our precious energy? Take out your journal. We are going to achieve clarity about the activities in your life that you need more of, versus the ones you need to let go of altogether.

When you awaken your star seed and flow in the river, you can learn to be quick and agile in order to make swift course corrections. Imagine you are in a small raft floating down rapids. It could be a thrill, full of joy and excitement, or it could feel really scary, like you are about to crash into a rock and drown. Choose your activities based on the feelings you want to experience.

I've developed a handy worksheet you can download on my website to guide you through this process: KnowTheSelf.com/workbook.

Below are eight questions to ponder:

1. Think of the things you do in a given day. What activities give you energy?

2. What activities deplete you?

3. What emotional situations give you energy?

4. What emotional situations deplete your energy?

5. Name the people in your life who give you energy?

6. Name the people in your life who deplete your energy?

7. List all the foods give you energy.

8. What foods deplete you or make you feel heavy and lethargic?

Once you understand what activities, situations, people, and food give you energy or deplete you, you can make wise choices about how you fuel yourself.

Also, notice whether your energy depletes those around you or enlivens them. How can you ensure that you are sourcing your own energy and supporting others from your overflow, rather than stealing energy from others? That was a trick question. The answer is: Vertical Alignment! I cannot express enough how vitally important it is that we become energy centers unto ourselves. When we source our own energy directly from the vertical plane, we can correct our energetic imbalances, seal our field, and create beautiful sustaining relationships.

When faced with difficult choices, sit still. Go into the center of your being and explore which choice gives you energy and which one drains you. Choose love over fear. Choose growth over stagnation. Choose liberation over enslavement. Choose truth over lies. Choose win-win over win-lose situations, and you will find yourself flowing freely in the river of life toward your divine destiny.

Pay attention to the lifestyle choices with which you are faced each and every day. How do you treat your belongings? What do you hold sacred, and what do you corrupt, abuse, or take for granted?

All our choices come into question when we begin to harmonize with the natural world. It is easy to judge other people and look outside yourself, but what is happening in your life? How do you treat the people, places, and things with which you interact each day? Look around your house. How do you treat your clothes, your car, or your kitchen? Do you live in beauty or chaos—or somewhere in between?

How can you make the space around you more beautiful? How can you align yourself with beauty and harmony? What do you need to let go of in order to make space for more beauty in your life? Is there something you can add to your morning or evening ritual to bring more harmony into your home and into your day? The answers to these questions are small steps you can take that will have a big effect on your psyche and your energetic body, and, by extension, on everyone around you.

Do you watch a lot of TV, listen to the radio, and read mainstream newspapers? If so, you are allowing your field to be conditioned and contaminated with a lot of fear, advertising, and the culture of corporate warfare of over-consumption, which breeds greed.

On a similar note, what music do you listen to? Does it put you in the flow? Does it uplift your soul and keep you centered? Or does it disturb your field, exaggerate your anger, or make you pine for things you don't have? Oftentimes the music we listen to, the advertising we are exposed to, and the places we shop feed our desires in a way that distracts and depletes us.

Take inventory of your life and make the necessary changes to align yourself with more beauty. Allow your divine essence to call the shots. Choose consciously!

Define New Measures

When my star seed warped into hyper-drive, I had to fully surrender to the fact that I was not (and am not) in control of my destination. Something bigger, wiser, and more supreme dictates my course of action. As I became the willing servant to the force of nature inside me, I realized the way I had been organizing my life no longer worked.

Having been really good at managing large-scale projects when I worked in tech, I loved planning for the future. But planning no longer works the way it used to for me. My future vision has shut off completely. The furthest into the future I have been able to plan has been three months. This has been frustrating, and I have fought this reality for many years. I finally gave up trying to plan. Well, I never really gave up planning for my future, but I continue to learn to surrender to living in the present flow.

When I attempt to plan something, I notice an energy in me grasping to create assurance and security. It is the energy of fear, which causes me to move ahead of myself, out of present time and into a place that isn't necessarily aligned with my divine destiny. In these moments, I've learned there are other things I am being asked to pay attention to first. What I really need to be doing is sitting still and trusting that the next steps will be shown right when I need them. And sure enough, the next step always appears just when I need it; no matter how many times this happens, it always surprises me.

Time and again, I have been shown that I will not fall flat on my face when I follow synchronicity and stay in present time. Even though I make what to my logical mind seem like wild choices, deep inside I know I am safe because I am being shown a magical path forward. This path only appears as I step forward, one step, and sometimes a few steps, at a time.

Another realization I had was that the rules I had clung to, or been programmed with, no longer applied to me. Suddenly there were exceptions to all kinds of rules, such that I found myself slipping through doorway after doorway. My mind became confused as I began trusting my heart. The choices I made didn't always look like wise or ethical choices to others. There were moments my mind was repulsed by my heart's decisions. A new set of rules and values began to govern my life. When I understood that I had created new rules and actually defined them for myself, I no longer found my mind and heart divided.

When you live in the flow of life, magical doorways open and it can be really confusing to know if going through them is the right thing to do. You will need to depend on your awakened heart to show you the way. Your alignment to your heart is the key to staying in the flow and living in harmony. If you have a lot of judgments about what is good and bad in the world, or right and wrong for other people, beware. Those judgments will need to be cleared in order for you to enter the river of life and meet your divine destiny. Those judgments will need to be stripped from you in situation after situation, until all that remains is your heart's true essence, until all that remains is love.

When life delivers massive challenges, jump on your cosmic surfboard and ride it out. You can find the through line, the pipeline that gets you out of the wave's destruction and into the fun of the challenge. It is exhilarating to ride the waves of life. We won't always make it through the pipeline before the wave breaks. Sometimes we crash and get tumbled in the wake. Like a brave surfer, get back on the board and try again!

In order to make the waves easier to ride, it's helpful to figure out what measures you want to use to define your success. These are your personal ethics and values. Not ethics and values that were determined on your behalf, but your personal rules to live by and ways you will measure yourself.

Grab your journal and answer the following questions:

1.   By what values do you define yourself? Is it the amount of money you make, how good you look, the accreditations you've received, or your relationship status? Be honest about all the ways you define yourself.

2.   Name at least six character traits you value the most in other people.

3.   What character traits do you value in yourself?

4.   What character traits do others value in you? (If you don't know, ask people.)

5.   Create a new list of values by which to measure yourself.

You can download these questions as a worksheet from my website: KnowTheSelf.com/workbook.

Keep your new list of values handy. Etch them in your mind. Pledge to use your own value system when making choices. In this way, you will be operating in right relation to your own ethics, values, and deeper soul knowing.

I've listed the value statements by which I like to measure myself. These are Native American values I have picked up along my path that have helped me find my way. Feel free to use these for your own measures, add to them, or edit them as you see fit.

The values I measure myself by:

- Live in impeccability, walk my talk, keep my promises.
- Live in harmony with myself and with others.
- Be in right relations, with Gaia and all that is.
- Recognize and realize the sacredness in all.
- Be a clear vessel, without shame or blame.
- Know that when I am giving, I am receiving; and in receiving, I am also giving.
- Love myself as a divine being.

It is important to stay agile when we flow in the river of life. This is not always easy when you are clinging to your fears. Try your best to allow life to happen *through* you rather than forcing your agenda on everything. We each have a control freak inside us who wants to steer the ship. Learning to trust in the unseen hand of your soul wisdom that is guiding you will make your journey more enjoyable. Determine your guiding lights, your values, ethics, and morals. These will act as your compass.

There is a beautiful river flowing. Allow it to carry you. The course to your divine destiny is always better than anything you can dream up. Learn to trust in the higher order of your soul's knowing and give yourself permission to enjoy the magical adventure. It is okay to be happy!

Witness the Second Sun

We live at a time when we are awakening to a New Earth. This New Earth I keep mentioning is the awakening of our multi-dimensional nature, the activation of our light bodies, and the remembrance of our true essence. This is happening both inside of us and outside of us.

Our time is one when greater and greater truth is being revealed, and it is alarming. Our government has been hiding truths from us for centuries and finally, many whistleblowers have felt brave enough to expose some huge cover-ups. People are beginning to see through the cracks of the hidden agenda. The agenda that manipulates us through organized religions, corporate governments, and a false democracy. The agenda that centralizes and manipulates our food supply. The agenda that monopolizes our natural resources, and covers up our galactic heritage is finally being exposed. We have made discoveries in technology that would solve many of the world's problems, yet those technologies and the people who invented them are being suppressed because they offer keys to the truth about our origins.

The ancient traditions speak of a second sun in our Universe, one that moves along on a much longer elliptical trajectory than our ordinary 365-day year. This longer cycle is called the "Great Year." It is the approximately 25,000-year cycle upon which both the Mayan and Vedic calendars are built. The second sun heralds the return of truth, what the Hindus refer to as the Golden Age, the *Satya Yuga*.

I believe I have already seen this second sun on the horizon and that this new era is already upon us. During a Vision Quest in the High Sierras of California, I sat outside without shelter, water, or food for five days, praying for a vision. The vision I kept seeing (as if on repeat) was two planets on the horizon. Each night before going to sleep, I would literally see the planet appear. It looked like two moons, but the words I heard again and again along with this vision were "second sun." This vision didn't make any sense to my logical mind, but soon after I returned from the Vision Quest, the pieces started to fall into place.

Before the Vision Quest, I had multiple premonitions about a time coming when the Earth would undergo cataclysmic change. In my meditative states, I was being trained to hold still for days on end. On one such occasion, I lay in the corpse pose for three days straight without eating, with very little water, and only a few trips to the bathroom. During those three days, my body was very heavy. I could not speak or move as the visions were being shown to me.

The main theme I kept seeing was that the Earth would soon go through a period of three days of total darkness, and I needed to learn not to move during this time. It was imperative to lie still, to act as if I were dead during the three-day process. I was told not to eat or speak but just to lie there and listen. When the sun returned (on the third day) I could stand up and go outside. However, what I saw emerging from the three days of darkness was a New Earth reality. Everything on the planet had been wiped clean.

The electrical systems we use now no longer worked, so there was no Internet or power. Our money was worthless. There was no way to communicate with phones or computers. In fact, our technology had disappeared altogether! I was standing in a landscape that looked like Earth, but all the manmade plastics and metal no longer existed. In these visions, there were very few people. I witnessed small communities rebuilding life in innovative ways that were in harmony with each other and with the Earth.

The sweetest part of my visions was when I was shown a birthing center. There, I saw a waterfall and fresh water springing up from the Earth. Women were gathered together and in sync with each other, laughing and singing, supporting each other in motherhood. There were small pools where women were lounging and bathing and birthing their babies. It was an extraordinary sight; it has been etched in my mind's eye. It plays like a movie anytime I remember it, just as real as it was the first time I saw it.

Soon after I returned from my five-day Vision Quest, I met a Native American woman who is the living oracle for her tribe. She shared with a small group of us the same vision that I, only days before meeting her, had experienced in my own meditations. She mentioned the imminent Earth changes and the three days of darkness. She told us not to move during the three days and that we should lie still. She told us not to eat, not to speak, and not to turn on lights or walk outside. She said people moving around will go crazy, there will be chaos and confusion everywhere on the surface of the Earth and that we should ignore all of it and stay indoors. She said it was imperative during these three days that we remain in place and maintain both deep inner and outer stillness.

What I saw in my Vision Quest in 2005, and in multiple meditations that took place from 2003 through 2005, was exactly what the Native Oracle came to share with me that day. Even though our visions and descriptions matched down to specific details, I had been unwilling to share this information with others—until now, that is. Fear of ridicule and skepticism kept me quiet. It feels important to share this with you now given everything that is going on in the world. These visions may in fact come to pass, and I feel it is necessary to prepare you for transcending the great shift.

There are many scientists speaking of the second sun, referring to it as Nibiru, or Planet X. There are rumors that NASA is hiding its imminent approach from us because it brings along with it a massive shift in consciousness. Some feel it is an actual planet. Others say it's a sun. Still others think it's a mothership. Whatever it is, it has a very strong magnetic power, and it is entering our Solar System. I have seen the second sun on multiple occasions with my eyes wide open. Watch the sunset or the sunrise, and you may also be able to see a second sun setting or rising along with our solar sun. What I was told in my meditation was that the second sun brings a new energy to our solar system. It will awaken our senses and activate our human potential. Sun gazing in the early morning or evening is a great way to take in this new solar energy.

When the second sun comes close, the Earth will enter a zero-point field, a reset point. We will experience super storms and solar flares that will wipe out all our electrical grids. If this comes to pass, do not join in the chaos, do not get excited, and do not tempt your fears. During this time, it is best to turn deeply inward and connect with your center in order to align. After the three days of darkness, the light will return, and we will enter into a higher vibrational field, a new dimension—the New Earth.

My visions showed me that this is the Christ Consciousness awakening in our hearts. The keys in this book will prepare you with what you need to stay grounded, centered, and aligned in your heart.

* * *

This is a wonderful time to be alive. We came here to participate in the most beautiful dance of light, one in which the darkness can be loved back into wholeness. As we wake up to our multidimensional nature, we will encounter new species that boggle our minds and ignite our senses. Our galactic friends already walk among us, and in the new world, we will know them more directly. Welcome them with love and peace in your hearts; there is no need to be afraid or subservient, for they are our peers and allies.

The work before you, the next step on your path, is to align your heart with love. As St. Bernard of Clairvaux told us in his famous sermon on the "Three Comings of the Lord," regarding the Third Coming of Christ:

> Fill your soul with richness and strength. Because this coming lies between the other two, it is like a road on which we travel from the first coming to the last. In the first, Christ was our redemption; in the last, he will appear as our life; in this middle coming, he is our rest and consolation.

This *middle coming* to which St. Bernard refers can very well be the awakening we are experiencing right now, in the center of our heart, in the remembrance of our divine nature. Be still and know that you are God!

Join Me

As you attune to your heart, you become a beacon and a magnifier for others to awaken and align in their proper placement on the golden Flower of Life Matrix. It is important that we tune our fields together to create a harmonic resonance in order to strengthen the golden thread and magnetize our soul groups. Do you want to join me in this mission? Here are a few ways to get involved:

Join the Mystery School: If you are ready to develop your Self Mastery, check out my courses and retreats. These take place online and in person throughout the year to assist you in activating your full potential.

Get Supported: If you are looking for customized support to heal soul wounds and return to wholeness, I open a few Soul Dive Sessions and Clarity Calls each month for specific cases. I also have a list of qualified peers with whom I work, and I would be happy to refer you.

Start Your Own Meditation Circle: Practice Vertical Alignment with your friends and family.

*Stay up to date with the cycles of the moon and my latest offerings by visiting my website and joining my inner circle: **KnowTheSelf.com***

Spread the Word!

As more people awaken their multidimensional nature, they will be seeking support and understanding. If someone you know is highly sensitive, empathic, or struggling with the harshness of the world, please give them this book or have them contact me through my website.

Teach children and young adults the Vertical Alignment exercise to keep them safe and enable them to stand as sovereign and free beings.

My prayer is that in small groups, we learn to align to this higher energy of love and slowly but surely re-stitch the fabric of humanity.

May all beings know love.

Download the Workbook

To download the worksheets and diagrams presented in this book, go to KnowTheSelf.com/workbook. In this companion workbook, you will receive a bundle of exercises to help you stay in the flow of synchronicity. Here is a list of the exercises you can expect to find in the workbook, along with additional resources for you:

- Vertical Alignment MP3 Guided Meditation
- How Balanced Is Your Life Worksheet
- Universal Laws
- Levels of Self-Mastery
- Grounding Illustration
- Vertical Alignment Illustration
- Understand Your Mental Makeup Worksheet
- Emotional Guidance Scale
- Positive Re-Patterning Worksheet
- Four Levels of Inner Growth
- Define New Measures Worksheet
- Discover Your Energy Flows Worksheet
- Design Your Ideal Day Worksheet
- Mindful Activity Monitor Worksheet
- Become a Sovereign Being Video
- A Playlist of High Vibe Music

Acknowledgments

I'd like to acknowledge those who held my hand, stood by me, and supported me through so much of my spiritual awakening: A-sha and Yamada-san, your guidance and love have taken me to the far reaches of the galaxy. May my work further your own mission and bring the golden network to life.

Blessings to my sister, whose struggle in life has made me tireless in my search for answers, may your pain become your power. May we soon find ourselves tending the garden of the New Earth together, knowing that love overcomes all pain. Thank you, Mom, for birthing me into being, for putting up with my wild antics, and for sticking with me when it challenged your deepest beliefs. Roger and Meri, your concerns, generosity, and love gave me confidence and peace of mind to muddle through multiple challenges. Paige and Alyse, your mere existence has inspired me to do my best to restore balance within and without. Mr. Fox, a.k.a. Adam Jacobowitz, your mischievous ways of teasing and testing trained me to rise to my greatest challenges instead of burrow back into hiding. In your weakness, you sharpened my sword. You were a perfect mirror. Thank you for the long hours you spent helping me edit this book to make this dream a reality. Without you, Tiger, this would not have been possible. May we self-actualize fully for the benefit of all beings. Allison and Teo, your care, open arms, and friendship gave me a safe landing and sanctuary to do this very important work. I am eternally grateful. Mark and

Cheri, thank you for being so active in my resurrection, on numerous occasions; for securing my future after the fire when I was in complete shock; and for supporting me with your creative genius. Your protection and care for me over many years has provided me safe haven and a sense of family.

A big thank you to all my near and dear ones: Vanya, Sky, Nomita, Tanya, aManda, Melitta, Zohara, Claudia, Chantal, Vivek, Barry and Stephon, Mayu and Franklin, Ameen and Selah, Arisa, Sahai, Bahareh, Natasha, Antonio, Arthur, Aunt Leeh, Steve B, Annah, DeAnna, Melissa, and Naia, Bianca, Belinda, Joanna, Vlad, Tenley, Naphtali, Danielle, Carmen, and Aubrey. Thank you all for being my loving support through all the trials, rebirths, and rememberings. It hasn't been easy. I commend your strength and honor your dedication and your mere ability to hang out with me.

A heartful thank you to my students, Nina, Kristin, Satya, Jane, and Paula who went the distance with me. To all the students of the Mystery School who diligently work on themselves, to my clients and to my supporters. I have learned so much from being a part of your journeys. Thank you for believing in me and for allowing me to share your innermost worlds. It has been an honor to serve you in your awakening process.

Thanks to my mentors—Takao Yamada, Mai A-sha Yamane, Vanya Orr, Dr. Chihiro Suematsu, Vivek Chaturvedi, Sue Anne Autrand, Claudia L'Amoreaux, Ken, Dr. Newton and Dr. Laxmi, Gurpreet Singh, Mark Matousek, and The Way of the Heart—for your guidance, love, and support in my awakening. A special thank you to the communities that have supported me and my work in the world: Impact Hub Oakland, The Shift Network, The Esalen Institute, The Bridget Center, The Earth Trust, Life University, Life Research Academy, Anjali Ashram, Ananda Pune, Pyramid Association of India, Pyramid Young Masters Association, The Lake House Temple, Balance Edutainment, The School of Ancient Wisdom, Symbiosis Events, GaiaField Network, Unify, Uplift, Global Congress of Spiritual Science, Ashland West African Dance Community and the Neoteric Crew. A special thank you to Stephen Dinan, Phillip Helmich, Chantal Monte, Kevens, Far I Shields, Mutima Imani, David and Kate Nichol, for your wisdom, personal council, and holding of deep presence. Your light helped me weather some big storms in 2015. Thanks to the Datla and Raju family for providing me a place to grow in my awakening, for caring for me when I fell ill, and for supporting my efforts and experiments. I bow to your patience, diplomacy, and unconditional love. You are great teachers. Thanks to Angela Lauria, Grace Kerina, Melissa Nations, and the entire team at Difference Press for believing in me, trusting me, and focusing me when I was facing absolute terror. Your safe container and your process provided the perfect platform and the community support I needed to make my dream of becoming an author a reality. Thank you Chet Turnbeaugh for wading through deep waters with me to restructure all that I was resisting! Thank you Annabelle, Robyn, Cynthia, Annabelle and Laura for being a part of my restructuring team; I could not have done this without you! I also want to thank my enemies, haters, and foes—without your resistance, I would not be able to gather my strength and remember my purpose. Thank you for challenging me; we are simply mirrors. And last, but not least, thank you, Japan, for awakening my sleeping memory, and thank you, India, for reclaiming me as your daughter. One day, I will return.

Know the Self

A Mystery School for Modern Day Living

(Photo credit: Hyunah Jang)

About the Author

Amelía Aeon Karris has been a way-seer and trend-setter throughout her career spanning technology, fashion, entertainment, intentional community design, and spirituality. In 1994, she co-founded one of the world's first web design companies, when most of the public had barely heard of email. What began as introducing people to cutting-edge digital and virtual realities has evolved into awakening people to their multi-dimensional natures.

Divine guidance has led Amelía to live a purposeful life at the edge of our collective evolution. Her entrepreneurial ventures led her to Japan and India, where she spent a decade working with those nations' elite business and spiritual leaders. She has seeded eco-communities in the USA and India, instilling her expertise in permaculture and community governance, and continues consulting with intentional communities today.

Amelía's powerful healing abilities and clear vision were forged during a series of spiritual initiations over a nine-year period that honed her multi-sensory awareness and unique voice. Her extensive past-life recall was noted in India, first placing her on national television and later addressing live audiences of as many as 60,000 spiritual seekers.

Over the last decade—through public speaking, teaching, and private counseling—Amelía has helped thousands of people liberate their minds, navigate spiritual awakenings, and live their divine destinies.

Her mission is to wake up humanity's sleeping potential, magnetize soul groups, protect psychic children, and traverse our present massive shifts in consciousness.

Made in the USA
Middletown, DE
31 August 2018